Ties That Bind

Scotland to Crete
A memoir by Marie Naxaki Karioti

Ties That Bind

Scotland to Crete
A memoir by Marie Naxaki Karioti

Edited by:
Sally Heard, Debra Papadinoff
and Eleanor-Mary Cadell

First Published in Greece 2012
© Marie Naxaki Karioti 2012

Second edition updated March 2012

The author's moral rights have been asserted.

Designed and typeset by
Douglas Foote

Printed in the UK by Lightning Source Ltd

ISBN 978-960-9610-03-2

Dedicated to my grandmother,
Jessie Elder Lindsay Couryer

Family Diagram

Robert Lindsay = Janet Elder

*James Lindsay | William Lindsay = Jane Horn | Lachlan Lindsay | Helen Lindsay | George Lindsay

Nellie Lindsay = ? Blain | Jane Lindsay | William Lindsay | George Lindsay = Margaret Nicoll | Robert Lindsay

Willie Blain | Charlotte Lindsay | Jessie Lindsay

William Lindsay

Jessie Lindsay = George Couryeraki

Nellie Couryeraki = George Naxaki

Jim Couryer = Peggy O'Hannon

Crystalie | Marie | Iolanthe Lindsay

Nellie

Ian | Janet

Marion | Patricia

Sarah | Tricia | Arthur | Molly | Rachel

Simon | Michael | Michella

*James Lindsay = Betsy Bell

Eva Themaki

George Lindsay

Nancy Lindsay

Nicoll Lindsay | Bruce Lindsay | William Lindsay

Ian | Allan | Eileen | Hazel | Roy | Eric | Brian | James | Simon | Wendy | Edward | John

Contents

i

Introduction

What made me begin to write an account of James Lindsay's life in Suda* in my late eighties? I feel I have to let my readers, relatives and others, know something about the circumstances that led to this little book.

From an early age I have been attracted to this story – my childhood was spent with my Granny Jessie in Lindsay House and when I was 16, Mother and I were in a shop belonging to my father's uncle in Hania. He turned to my mother and said, "As long as Marie lives, Jessie will not die". These words marked my life. I was to be the keeper of the Scottish past in my life and the Cretan branch of the Lindsays of Dundee.

Then came the war, with the German occupation, the eviction of my family from Bella Vista and the loss of James Lindsay's mementos to the sea. Much more was dropped into the sea that day, including a ping-pong set, still unopened, which had been given to my sisters and me.

Apart from the time spent with Mother when she was old and living in Athens, when the Scottish past came to mind, I had little thought of writing the old story. I never missed regular visits to Crete over the years, visiting my cousins in Suda and Lindsay House (now in the hands of strangers). But for many years my time was otherwise occupied.

* Old spelling of Souda

There was a time when I started a collection of Greek crochet lace, which now comprises 800 pieces. As a matter of fact, the collection started in Crete and took me to many parts of the mainland and islands; it is now housed in a folk museum in Plaka in Athens.

I also made a great many pencil drawings, especially during the years of my marriage, when I spent so much time in Arcadia, Peloponnese, and at my husband's family home in Leondari.

In 1990 my husband died after a long and painful illness. I went back to his home in Arcadia, but I was holidaying for longer periods of time in Hania.

I then moved on to another interest: the *Sfakiot* finger-lace edging of the handwoven *petseta* runner. I was alone and back in Crete, which is what I needed: to be in Crete to look up at the White Mountains and across the sea.

A couple of years ago, I got a surprising phone call. Two cousins, Roy and Eric Lindsay from Dundee, wished to meet me. On a visit to Scotland, when Eric met me in Inverness, I learned so much more about the Lindsay story and they, too, from me.

In 1999 I moved to Crete and at last could sit on the steps of Lindsay House and feel the presence of the old folk. It was just a matter of taking up pen and paper. I posted what I had written to Eric, chapter by chapter. When all the chapters had been typed by Eric, he handed on my typescript to Roy, who found it very interesting. He corrected any facts I had got wrong and added more photos. Now, after a final edit, this is the result.

As the news of the story spread through the family, more and more descendants of the Lindsays were visiting Crete, interested in discovering their past: Roy and Eric, Simon (Nancy's son from Australia) and, of course, my cousins

Marion and Tricia, and their brother Lindsay's daughter, Janet, from South Africa. I think we are all happy that this little book has been written.

I would like to thank Mr Potamitakis for his valuable information on the Arsenal and docks of Suda. I thank Manolis Bousakis for checking the political facts I mention about Crete. I also thank Manolis Manousakas, who kindly lent me several Suda photographs taken at the time James Lindsay resided in Crete.

Also, my dear friend and artist, Sally Heard for copying, correcting and editing my work, to Debra Papadinoff for reading it through, and to Eleanor-Mary Cadell for the final edit and corrections while she was visiting me in Hania from South Africa.

After a long, interesting and precious life, at the age of 94, I still look back with love and wonder at my early life with Granny Jessie at Lindsay House and the entire saga of my Scottish/Cretan family.

As I look back on the recent past, I see there are a few events in my immediate family that I would like to include. The presence of Simon in our lives has been a great joy! Simon has written a short account of his personal search and 'discovery', which will be included in this book. I will only say that he had eight close years with his mother, Nancy, who died suddenly while Simon and his family were spending a holiday in Crete.

Another separation was the death of Cathrine Lindsay, Nancy Payne and, even more recently, the death of my own beloved sister, Iolanthe. But happily there are babies connected to my story: Kayla's baby little Jessie; a baby boy to Jan in South Africa named Mitchell James Lindsay Couryer; Rachel's baby girl called Lottie – Simon's first grandchild.

Meanwhile, I too am getting on in years. I enjoy being in Crete in the middle of March when the swallows come back to Crete, as they have always done, while in February the little blue and pink anemones push through the soil and lift their little faces to the winter sun: as I look down I hear them whisper *'love me'* and I am contented.

Marie Naxaki Karioti

Foreword

In the millennium, 2000, I asked my brother if he would like to join me on holiday in Crete. It would be an autumn break for both of us, with mountain walking as its main objective. "Yes", he said. "That sounds great". In the past we had enjoyed walking holidays together on other Mediterranean islands such as Majorca and Corsica, but never Crete.

However, on this occasion I had an ulterior motive. I had been rooting through our family box of photographs in 'Suda', our joint holiday home (it had been our parents' and grandparents' home, but they had long since passed away). It was in Wormit, Fife, Scotland. I had come across some photos that intrigued me.

One photo was of a child, a baby, lying face down on a cushion. The photo was sepia. It had on the reverse, in neat copper-plate writing: 'Crystalie Naxaki, born 10 July 1915' and was taken in Manchester. Perhaps it was the coincidence that it was the date between my brother's birthday and mine, 9th and 11th July, that drew my attention to the photo, or perhaps it was because I could not understand why such a picture should be in our collection. What was the connection between this photograph and our family?

The second photo, also sepia and even older, was of a gravestone, very grand, and with the inscription below:

James Lindsay
Born Dundee, Scotland, 14 Sept 1824
Died Suda Bay, 17 May 1899
&

Elizabeth Bell
Wife of above
Born Glasgow, 8 July 1813
Died Halepa, 8 Feby 1900
"Blessed are the dead who die in the Lord"

The intriguing detail was that relatives of ours were buried in Suda in Crete. What was the connection? I knew that our grandmother was from Crete, and that she had asked that her ashes be spread in Suda Bay when she died. I knew that my grandfather, George John Lindsay, and his daughter, Nancy, had travelled out to Crete to fulfil her wishes after she died in 1951, but that was long after the dates of either photograph. That was the extent of my knowledge.

So, in September 2000, my brother Eric and I embarked on a holiday to Crete and booked in to a self-catering apartment in Platanias, 8 miles west of Hania, the old Cretan capital, and 11 miles west of Suda. Eric and I knew that we'd have the opportunity to do some great gorge walks on the south coast of Western Crete, and we set our hearts on the Samaria Gorge, if weather permitted. I also mentioned that I'd take the two pictures along and if we had a wet day we could perhaps do some family research. Little did I know what would unfold!

This book is about a man who was born in 1824 and died in 1899 – James Lindsay, an architect, engineer and dock builder, a self-made man, who travelled from Scotland to

Constantinople and thence to Crete, where he retired and continued his love affair with that wonderful and captivating island.

From the opening to the introduction you may be forgiven for making the mistake of thinking that this book is an hisorical perspective about an obscure fellow of long ago, but you would be quite wrong. It is a remarkable tale told by a remarkable woman, who has spanned four generations, has memorised the tales of her family from the previous three generations, and is venerated by all her known living relatives.

Marie Karioti is now ninety-four, but she writes with clarity and a memory that has not been dulled by the years. In fact, she admits that her memories are clearer now than they have ever been. I find her a fascinating companion, delightful company and always with depths yet unplumbed. She has a cheeky and even mischievous nature and I imagine she was a very naughty child – always testing the limits of her parents, and even now this side of her character comes through in her writing.

Marie now lives in a penthouse flat in Hania. It's a bright, breezy location, with a view to the south over the White Mountains and a view to the north over the Bay of Hania, towards mainland Greece. On my last visit she displayed her family photos, sepia and well thumbed, with delight as she related gems of family history. She cherishes the Cretan characteristics of liberty and freedom. *"I must get it down on paper before it's too late"*, she said, *"whilst it's all still so vivid"*. Then she drifted off down memory lane, weaving a tapestry of family events much like the lace she so lovingly creates. On 8 August 2007 Marie exhibited her lace work at the age of ninety – what a woman! *"It's been such a busy year, so eventful; I think I'll write a book about it."*

James Lindsay is a major player in the book, but there are so many other richly characterised players that your attention will be constantly absorbed and the book will carry you forward on a rollercoaster of tales from one generation to another. The book covers the family history up to the present day. As a family record of history Marie's story is absorbing, a must for budding Lindsay family historians.

Roy F Lindsay

Chapter I

Bella Vista in 1942

Mother walked into the long cool storeroom, one of three in the basement of Bella Vista, the Naxaki family home. The storeroom was always cool because of a cistern of rainwater above, collected from the roof tiles down a drain. A tap installed below on the sloping garden provided us with fresh rainwater. One of the other two rooms was a large wash house containing a built-in oven nd cauldron for heating water for the monthly wash, a well with brackish water and two concrete tubs, one large and one small. The washroom was dark, with only the door letting in light: this room was built on to the rock face. The third storeroom was square, large and always untidy. There were rows of shelves around the walls with pots of paint, brushes, ladders, fishing tackle and gardening utensils, cases of old clothes, shoes and broken furniture. A window let in daylight, making a good playroom for us in our early years, especially on a rainy day. When the fear of German occupation became a reality, my father dug a bomb shelter out of the rockface and lined it with stone benches and cushions.

In the room where Mother stood were two large demijohns standing on wooden boards, filled with red and white wine, our annual supply purchased from local villages. A large earthenware jar, known as a pythos, stood in the upper corner, filled with olive oil. Plenty of daylight and fresh sea air came from a decorative wrought-iron framed skylight. Against one wall was a rough wooden crate, one and a half metres high and more or less a metre wide. I remember the height because as a little girl of nine or ten, I lifted the lid, which was attached to hinges, and leaned it against the wall, which allowed me to examine the contents. I remember seeing a grey sepia oblong ledger book without a cover, written in faded pink and spidery letters across the ruled pages in columns of pounds, shillings and pence which, of course, meant nothing to me except to pique my curiosity.

Mother stood and pondered. Our home, Bella Vista, had to be vacated within twenty-four hours. Upstairs my father and my sisters, Crystalie and Iolanthe, were busy packing with friends and relatives who had come to help. My father was packing his telescope, microscope and 13 volumes of the British *Encyclopaedia Britannica*, 1913 edition, printed on rice paper. Crystalie was packing her books and Iolanthe her toys, including her favourite Chinese doll, Chen Fou Po, and her furry clown monkey.

Mother's pride had been cruelly hurt the day before. Rumours had been circulating that a German Gestapo search was to take place at our house, though no one knew exactly when. It was believed that someone had given information to the Gestapo in exchange for a favour, denouncing my father and his two brothers as Anglophiles and stating that my father, George, had been passing information to British submarines passing close to the shores of Bella Vista. All three homes were searched by the Gestapo on the same day.

Their first port of call was my Uncle Kyriakos' home, which was a typical Cretan house. Although nothing was found, during their search the Gestapo sliced through a painting of a large portrait of Eleftherios Venizelos, apparently in the hope of finding British gold sovereigns hidden behind the canvas.

At the home of my Uncle Kostas, my father's youngest brother, a conversation was struck up in German between my uncle and the Gestapo. Not that Uncle Kostas was any less their enemy, but he had visited Germany in the past and attended a Hitler Youth Rally. He had a good command of German and at the beginning of the occupation had been able to save the lives of some Cretans and his own family, in a village where many of the male inhabitants had been lined up against the wall to be shot by German soldiers.

The Gestapo arrived at Bella Vista during the day. They locked my father and sisters (I was ill in the sanatorium with TB) in one of the upstairs bedrooms and my mother accompanied them on their search of the house. On the upper landing wall hung a large print of 'The Monarch of the Glen', which must have come from Lindsay House in Suda. They moved in to my father's study and showed surprise at the number of English books, although embarrassed as they opened and shut drawers under my mother's stern watch. My mother, half-Scottish and half-Cretan, carried herself with pride and dignity, and should an officer have pulled his gun, she would have remained motionless and defiant.

Looking back, I imagine the Germans must have despised but tolerated the Cretans. They had lost many young parachutists shot down over Maleme or killed on the fields by locals carrying guns, sticks and knives – a battle they had not expected. The reprisals were harsh. The resistance on Crete had delayed Germany's planned attack on Russia, and the cold Russian winter further delayed their advance.

But to return to my father's study on that terrible day at Bella Vista: the Gestapo failed to find his diary, in which, if they had, they would have read:

> *April 6th–Germany and Italy attack Greece;*
> *retreat of Greek army. 80,000 British in great*
> *flight, 30,000 arrive in Crete. Miss Burgess and*
> *Miss Hern stopped with us for two days.*
> *April 29th–Left for Egypt, under bombing!*

Neither did they find Crystalie's pencilled note:

> *Parachutists rounded up on small bridge,*
> *troops both sides of the gully. Mr Savage called*
> *at 'L', looks shaken after three narrow escapes;*
> *one at the ARP post, another in the mess and a*
> *third outside our house.*

Nor did they thoroughly search the wardrobe in my parents' bedroom. In the far corner under my father's winter coat hung the Rev. H. Savage's official uniform, missing his hat, which my sister Crystalie, had filled with stones and thrown into the sea before the Gestapo arrived, to be lost forever. Above all of this, however, was the terrible loss of the house, Bella Vista, and the realisation that our beautiful home would be occupied by our enemy, the invaders of Crete.

When the Gestapo had completed their search of Bella Vista, the verdict was harsh. We had to vacate and empty the property within 24 hours. We were given a small house in Hania's old town, where we were to move with all our belongings.

Bella Vista was a two-storey house with six bedrooms, two spacious living rooms and three large storerooms, facing a sea that stretched as far as mainland Greece. The house was big and full of furniture and belongings collected over the years and many things brought from Manchester and Lindsay House in Suda Bay, including my Great Uncle Lindsay's personal crate, which it is believed contained books, ledgers, charts and diaries. How was it that the contents of the crate came to Bella Vista and why? James Lindsay died in 1899 and his wife Betsy a year later. Maggie Montgomery, Betsy's niece, died in 1917 and, following the death of Maggie, Lindsay House was solely occupied by Jessie Lindsay Couryer and her family.

But on that particular day, Mother was in despair as she stood looking down into the crate. Its contents were British and Britain was at war with Germany. My mother knew she had to protect her husband and children and she did not want the Germans seizing these personal and private papers. In a desperate act, she bent down into the crate and gathered up an armful of its contents, then marched out of the storeroom and along the courtyard to the wall that towered above the sea below. She opened her arms wide and let go. As they fell into the sea, the heavier books sank to the bottom and the lighter papers floated away on the crest of the waves. With her heart pounding, she knew deep down inside she was doing the right thing and, repeating her actions over and over again, she finally emptied the entire contents of the crate into the sea. She then went calmly upstairs to help the others pack.

By evening there was still a lot to do. Someone arrived at the front door and my mother looked down the stairs from the landing above. The Rev. Johan Mathies stood looking up at her. (Rev. Mathies was the Methodist chaplain for the local German barracks. On arriving in Hania, he had enquired about the existence of a non-conformist Protestant congregation. With a fluent command of the English language, he had made acquaintance with my family and became a good friend to many Cretans.) "How you must hate us," he called up to my mother. Mother replied with a plea: "Please get them to give us another 24 hours: there is so much to clear out, we simply can't manage".

A little later the Reverend returned to Bella Vista with an extension of 24 hours. He later told us that the Germans had been annoyed with him at headquarters for being too friendly with the Cretans and that he would have to stop intervening. The following day we moved out of Bella Vista.

We never returned to Bella Vista. For the past 60 years the house has been occupied by other people, mostly friends. I have visited them often and I always feel their presence in the house but never that of the German Army. Is it that we remember only what we want to, or is it that the Germans never left their mark? Even when they left Bella Vista it was not handed back to us but to the United Nations Repatriation Authority (U.N.R.A.).

Many years later and on many occasions I asked Mother what the wooden crate had contained. She always answered, "Oh, just bills and accounts", and I would go on asking her again and again. It has been an obsession of mine. If only I could go back in time, I would draw up a chair, open the lid and carefully catalogue everything I believe to have been inside. And I would read and read and read. I would then have been able to write a straightforward account of the life of James Lindsay. Those documents had not been thrown out from Lindsay House but brought to Bella Vista for safety.

After a long absence I have finally returned to Crete, where James Lindsay lived and loved over a century ago. Now I can wander around Lindsay House; I can walk the road he walked; I can look up at Malaxa and the White Mountains as he once did.

Over the years many of the Lindsay family have been coming back to Crete, each one attracted by something they had heard in childhood or read in a letter kept in an old leather portfolio of a family connection between Dundee and Suda Bay in Crete.

Granny Jessie had many stories to tell and told them over and over again. I know them all and hope to relate them as I remember. My mother Nellie was more reserved. She put off talking about the past until it was too late. For me, over all these years, the Lindsay story has been a part of me, it is my own. Mother would have said of me that I have a vivid imagination and half the things I say are all in my mind.

I have the story in my mind and it is all in sepia! All the photographs we have, either taken in Dundee or Hania, are in sepia. So I have coloured Lindsay House and its story. I want to gather all those people in the photographs and get close to them. I want to write of their joys and sorrows here in Crete and elsewhere; to write about their contentment here on this beautiful island, their deep nostalgia for the land of their birth and the years spent in the Mediterranean climate. I will try not to digress too much but will keep the figure of James Lindsay to the fore.

Two years ago, in Dundee, two Lindsay brothers picked up an old photograph of a gravestone, which they had found in a collection of old documents, letters and photographs. On the gravestone was carved 'James Lindsay–Born Dundee, 14 September 1824, Died Suda Bay, 17 May 1899'. So they travelled to Crete in search of an old namesake.

Arriving in Hania, they drove to the municipality offices in Suda. The girl at the desk looked at the photograph and shook her head in disbelief, she then made a telephone call and a few hours later I met Roy and Eric Lindsay, great-grandnephews of James Lindsay, for the first time. We began talking and I have now decided to write.

James Lindsay and his wife Betsy (née Bell) had no children of their own. James's brother William and wife Janet (née Horn) had six children. Their offspring are scattered in Canada, USA, South Africa, Australia, New Zealand, England and, most of all, Scotland and Greece.

Their descendants are taking their time, but slowly they are coming back to Crete because they know they have roots here. They hear of the connection between Dundee and Suda Bay and they want to know more.

Will I be able to give some life to the story of long ago, involving all those figures in the sepia photographs? Will I get help in the way of a letter, a document, a picture, an old piece of lace or an oral remembrance?

Chapter 2

James Lindsay –
Dundee, Constantinople, Crete

I am trying to write about someone's life, yet I have no information regarding his early years. I have his date of birth and hardly anything else. Yet I think I know what James Lindsay looked like at the age of seven, when he first attended school: a sturdy boy, in a thick brown tweed suit and knee-length trousers, black hand-knitted woolly socks that reached his knees and wearing highly polished boots. His satchel with his slate, copy book and chalk was made of thick material.

James Lindsay was the first-born of Robert and Janet Lindsay. Five years later his brother Lachlan was born, although there is nothing known of him. His name is in a register, but there is no mention of him in the family records. I don't know when he died; it could have been in childhood. In 1831, a brother named William was born; I know him well because he was my great-grandfather! Helen, the only girl, was born in 1833. I have a sepia photograph of her with her parents, probably taken at the time she was engaged to be married. Her dowry was complete, containing some dainty silver spoons made in the design of a shell. Sadly, she died before her wedding and her dowry must have been given out among members of the family because my sisters and I were eventually given one of the silver spoons each. The youngest brother, George, was born in 1837, but he also fades into the background, though the name George appears in the family for the next three generations.

The Lindsay family's occupation is interesting. In the various registrar's certificates we see a mention of 'Weavers', 'Potato Merchants', 'Tea Dealers' and 'Grocer'. There is a photograph of the Potato Merchant's store: a Lindsay in his top hat and carriage and the workmen and women standing around the entrance under a large sign, which reads 'Potato Merchants'. There is also a funny story from this time, although told much later when William Lindsay was married and had a grown-up daughter, Jessie, my grandmother. The story tells how Jessie went to see her father at the store one day, accompanied by a young man who respectfully asked for her hand in marriage. My dour great-grandfather looked at the young man and then pointed at a nearby sack of potatoes and said, "You can have that!" One of many of Jessie's love affairs that went amiss!

We know that the Lindsays had hand-looms for weaving linen and that when mechanical looms came into force, their businesses failed. Was this when they moved in to the potato and tea industries? I have two tiny tea cloths with drawn threads and trimmed in crochet lace, which I believe Jessie either made herself or had made by someone in Suda. The crochet lace is in a Cretan design and one of the tea cloths I have given to Eric.

But let us return to the young James Lindsay, on his way to school on a rainy day in Dundee. He had been born during a very interesting period in Scottish history. I have been reading a little history from the end of the 18th and beginning of the 19th centuries, which was a period of great achievement and great poverty. The soil of Scotland was poor and families were large: due to poverty and hunger, many children died in infancy. The story of the evictions and clearances is very familiar, but with the appearance of the potato, peasants became better nourished and there was an improving medical care system, enabling children to reach adulthood. The result of this was a great increase in the population, which subsequently led to more voluntary emigration.

At the other end of the social scale Scotland was flourishing. In architecture, Edinburgh was called the 'Athens of the North'. Scottish universities became renowned, with an increase in the study of Medicine, Law, Engineering and Literature. Robert Burns wrote his poetry and sang his songs. Walter Scott wrote his wonderful novels. Portrait painting became the fashion. Who isn't familiar with the great painters and paintings of that period, such as 'The Reverend Robert Walker skating on Duddingston Loch', by Henry Raeburn? Doctors and engineers were becoming well known beyond the boundaries of Scotland. In Russia and Turkey, Scottish names filled eminent posts and many Scots could be found in the military, on expeditions and as missionaries. Success overseas and a natural wanderlust sent Scotsmen all over the globe. There was achievement in many ventures, from poor bedraggled emigrants to the well-to-do professionals. As ship-building, technology and science developed, more Scots, both at home and abroad, became eminent figures. *'Scottish names are the brightest stars in the firmament'*– J.D. Mackie, *History of Scotland.*

The Lindsays of Dundee belonged to the middle-class. They were not destitute emigrants or famous names in history. The potato industry was the backbone of Dundee.

The Dundee Lindsays were well fed, well clad and the children were given an education. However, it appears that only James Lindsay went to university. The family home was comfortable, although not by today's standards. Morning prayers and Kirk attendance on Sundays were compulsory.

The Lindsay family, like many of their class, visited the local photographers, whilst Robert and Janet Lindsay had their portraits painted. Robert looks like Gladstone: black suit, watch and chain, a venerable figure of his time, while his wife Janet is a rather unattractive, plump and heavy-lidded elderly lady in a bonnet with a large brooch pinned on to the collar of her tight-fitting bodice. We were always told, rather apologetically, that her portrait had been painted from a photograph after her death.

By the time James had completed his studies in engineering at The Watt Institute in Dundee, the family had grown in number and there were now other priorities. It was time for him to look out for himself. At this time he could have found work in Scotland, but I am afraid that now I have to do some guesswork. What age had he reached? Twenty? He knew of faraway places and the possibility of success abroad. In *The Life of the Lindsays,* by Sir Alexander Lindsay, there is mention of the Rev. Henry Lindsay, who was Chaplain to the British Embassy in Constantinople around 1857 and author of several books.

Did James and the Rev. Lindsay know each other? They may have met later in Constantinople, or perhaps the Turkish Government had sent out requests for professionals. We know that Germans, or rather Prussians, trained the Turkish army. Engineering, however, was in the hands of the British and Turkey has always been in a position to take advantage of Western European knowledge and culture. Whether he was invited to go or not, Turkey was James's destination. He would have had to face the cost of travelling and at this time he married Betsy Bell, who was 11 years his senior. Did she have the money?

I think I will have to stop asking myself questions with no hope of any answers; I will just relate my story as I see it in my mind's eye. Since I was a child of six, I have lived with stories of Uncle Lindsay, his wife and their life together, the latter part of which was spent in Suda, Crete. How deeply rooted these stories are no one but myself knows.

Through my long life there have been periods when my daily affairs permitted little thought of the past, but those memories were recurrent: my childhood with Granny in Lindsay House and later my companionship with my mother in her old age in Athens, when we would sit and chat, with her sitting in her large armchair, the sepia photographs brought out from time to time to once again remember names and relationships from the past. And now, above all, when I have returned to Crete and can visit Lindsay House at any time, with its gathered memories as old as 141 years, from 1868-2011, it's all quite incredible! In other families there are boxes and boxes of letters, in mine there are none: Mother, alas, saw to that! If I were younger, I would visit Constantinople and do some serious research. However, as it is, I will just tell my own story as I remember and at times use my imagination.

James Lindsay made up his mind to travel east to Constantinople, with no doubt of securing an engineering post when he arrived. Later, in 1860, his father Robert left him a property in Dundee, but at the time he may not have been able to help James financially or perhaps he did. Now married to Betsy Bell, James set out for Constantinople. How did the couple travel: overland across Europe? No, that was the route the wealthy took, in a 'carriage and four' on what was named 'The Grande Tour'. It would most likely have been from Scotland via London and on board one of the new steamships that chugged up and down the east coast. He would have loaded his large wooden trunk on board, which is still in the family and has a story of its own.

The trunk was taken to Bella Vista from Lindsay House. It stood in our summerhouse against the window as a seat, painted blue with blue and white cushions. Crystalie and I had decorated the summerhouse with dolphins and sailors, stencilled and painted. Some years later, when the summerhouse was redecorated with a frieze of painted tulips around the walls and a floral interior, the trunk was painted red and used again as a seat. I remember kneeling on it and leaning out of the window, watching the sea and daydreaming not of Uncle Lindsay, but of my own future. I wish I could have told that young girl that years later she would be in Crete writing her family saga. When I went to Athens the trunk went with me – this time painted green, the colour it has remained. From home to home in Athens, the trunk went with me. In my last Athenian home, in Aradou Street, I used it as a stand for my music centre. My niece, Nellie, now has the trunk in the same apartment and uses it as a surface for her books and papers. Although I have a number of items from Lindsay House, I have always cherished Uncle Lindsay's trunk as once being one of his most personal belongings.

So, James and Betsy Lindsay boarded the ship in Scotland, he with his trunk and she with her hatboxes. They were sailing to Byzantium: south from Scotland down the Bay of Biscay, a rough voyage through the straits of Gibraltar into the Mediterranean and past the Greek islands. At one point they would have sailed past the north coast of Crete. Little did they know that one day they would return to the island to make a happy home. The ship then turned north to the eastern coast of the Dardanelles and the Bosporus. At this point they would have had their first glimpses of one of the most beautiful capitals of the world, Constantinople, with its golden church domes and pencil-shaped minarets pointing high above the city and the smell of spices from the East reaching their nostrils. I wish I could have stood beside them as they landed on that strange shore without a word of Greek or Turkish, to have witnessed what they did and where they went. I have been reading a book on Constantinople in the middle of the 19th century. It was the most cosmopolitan city in the world, with a long troubled history, governed by the Turks with large communities of Greeks, Jews, Armenians and Europeans.

Who met them? Where did they go with their trunk and hatboxes? What year was it, 1848 or 1850? What a land and sea: the Sea of Marmara, the Bosporus, the Black Sea, the Golden Horn and the coast of Asia Minor, opposite Galata and the Princes Islands! The 1850s were an important period in Turkish history. The land and people were wealthy and merchandise travelled from East to West through her ports: spices, fabrics, minerals and products from the East. More and more foreigners made their way to Constantinople. Embassies of every country set up in the great city, along with bankers and consuls, among them the Rev. Henry Lindsay. It was a time when the Sultan was either 'out of popularity' or under European pressure to implement 'equal rights' for the city's multi-cultural citizens. Christian church bells were allowed to ring and Greek culture allowed to flourish.

I have one interesting date from my reading of a little history. In 1847-1849 two Swiss brothers were employed by the Sultan to make some repairs to the church of Agia

Sophia. When old plaster was removed from the walls, life was once gain given to magnificent mosaics. James and Betsy must have visited and admired these masterpieces.

I read a detailed description of the main street Pera, known as Grande Rue de Pera, where some fifty percent of the shops were run by Greeks and where the Catholic Church of St Antonio stood. The spice market was the most celebrated in the East and the architecture reflected many cultures, wooden houses with protruding wooden balconies and 'peepholes', where women could sit and watch the world go by. I also read one detail that caught my attention: the roofs of the houses had a sheet of lead under the tiles. Was this a form of insulation? Many years later when James Lindsay was building Lindsay House, he too used a sheet of lead under the tiles, which was discovered when the Germans bombed Suda and the top storey of the house was damaged. There is little doubt that the young James Lindsay would have improved his skills in Constantinople.

Where did he live for all those years up until 1869, when he finally set sail for Crete? My research reveals that the Europeans preferred to make their homes on the Thracian Bank of the Bosporus and that one of these buildings was used as the British Embassy, and along the coast was a row of beautiful villas with their foundations washed by the Marmara Sea, an area that was apparently home to the foreign embassies of Britain, Spain, France and others.

It was with the passing of the 'Equal Rights' bill that great development flourished in literature and the arts. The Greek Literary Association of Constantinople, including the Academy, the University and the Ministry of Education, was inaugurated in 1861 and James Lindsay was there!

General information like this is easy to write, but what exactly did James Lindsay do in Constantinople from the time he reached the city to the time the Turkish Government sent him to Crete to build the great Arsenal in Suda? This is my great query! Once, when my very reserved and rather silent mother, by then in her eighties, felt she should pass on information she knew of the family saga, she told me one day: "James Lindsay built the harbour of the Bosporus". Those were her very words, but what did that mean exactly? Perhaps Mother felt, seeing my anxiety for knowledge of the past, that she should not have so hastily emptied the contents of the wooden crate into the sea at Bella Vista.

The Lindsays must have spent about fifteen years in Constantinople. James would have learned Turkish and some Greek, too. From their Turkish home I still have the lower part of an opaline glass lamp, pale green and white, very lovely, a soup tureen, a single piece from a dinner set in grey and white with a light brown meander design. There is also a plate with some ivy leaves (but that could have come from Scotland) and an earthenware pot that might have been used to store lard or ginger.

There are no photographs of James and Betsy in Turkey. Did they, during that time, return to visit Dundee? But there is one more beautiful memento: Aunt Betsy's oriental shawl in very fine silk with a black fringe, which had been kept by Granny Jessie and handed down to my mother, Nellie.

But let's go back to James Lindsay's duties in Constantinople. I have recently been talking to Mr Potamitakis, a local historian, who has been researching and writing about the history of Suda and, naturally, the building of the docks and Arsenal are included in his writing. It was he who, two years ago, when a group of the Lindsay offspring came to Crete and we arranged an evening meal together with our Couryeraki cousins at a seafront restaurant, took us all round the Arsenal wall and buildings, explaining what was old and what was new. Once more my strong desire for knowledge of the past flared up and since then he and I have had several meetings.

This is what he wrote:

> *'As far back as the Egyptian invasion of Crete, the ground by the sea in Suda had already been selected as the appropriate location for the Arsenal. Work on it had been going on at a very slow pace, until 1869 when the Turkish Government sent the Scottish architect and engineer James Lindsay, who had been responsible for the building of the Bosporus Harbour, to build the Arsenal. James Lindsay, with his experience and architectural knowledge of the time, planned, supervised and brought to completion the work.'*

The above paragraph is in the Suda Naval archives. Mr Potamitakis also told me that it would be quite useless searching for more information about Constantinople, as the Turks were very secretive about giving any details out about their past political history.

So, in 1869, James and Betsy were to leave their home and friends in Constantinople and move to Crete. I think I can say for certain, from the above reference, that James Lindsay must have been held in great esteem by the Turkish Government to be entrusted with the building of the great Arsenal at Suda. I wonder what the now middle-aged couple, with no family of their own, felt about this sudden change in their lives. Their life in such a cosmopolitan capital as Constantinople must have been pleasant if not exciting; yachting, sailing and fishing, attending club events and embassy functions with a large British and foreign community. Had they mixed well with the high society of Constantinople? Did Betsy wear her silk shawl at evening parties? Oh dear, the questions I want to ask!

Once again, James Lindsay packed his trunk and Betsy her finery and household goods and furniture. Would they have sailed by ship directly from Constantinople to Hania, Crete? Oh dear, I am so glad they did so, otherwise where would I be, with this wonderful story of my Scottish ancestors whose genes are surely in me? Their memories have accompanied me in my long life. I want all my cousins, little cousins and even littlest cousins, to know of their Cretan connection with Scotland: two lands and cultures that joined hands in Suda Bay.

Chapter 3

Crete – History and Politics

In 1869 the Sultan Abdul Aziz in Constantinople asked James Lindsay to go to Suda, Crete, to complete the building of the great Arsenal. The plans for the Arsenal had been drawn up some time previously by the Egyptians.

The Arsenal was inaugurated in 1872. It comprised a number of buildings to house the administration, personnel, workshops and a hospital. For security reasons, the road side of the complex was surrounded by a high stone wall.' The buildings inside the Arsenal may have changed over the years, but the wall is still a picture of good 'Scottish' architecture, as it stands strong as ever after 150 years. I remember, as a child with my sisters and Mother, walking along beside the wall, when my mother removed a dried white, delicately designed discarded skin of a serpent from a crevice in the wall. As mentioned earlier, it was in 2001 that Mr Potamitakis took Roy and Eric Lindsay and I on a guided tour of the great Arsenal.

Within a paragraph, I have touched on three dates: the near-completion of the great Arsenal in 1872; the discarded serpent skin in 1927; and the visit of two members of the

Lindsay Clan in 2001. Time means little when you have a story to tell, you go from one memory or fact to another, like stepping stones. I am now standing at the threshold of 2005 and I want to go on with the story I began last year. The important thing is that I am living on the very land where all this happened so long ago.

So there was now a great change taking place in the lives of James and Betsy Lindsay. Did they realise how different their lives would be in Crete after the splendour of Constantinople?

In April 1865, Edward Lear travelled to Crete and gives us an account in his 'Cretan Journal'. As the Lindsays arrived only four years later, I will give you Lear's account, which, I am sure, could not have been that different from James Lindsay's. The Lloyd Triestino Austrian line made the voyage every fortnight from Trieste to Constantinople via Syra to Crete. Edward Lear came from Corfu via Syra to Hania.

'Boarded the 'Persia' (Austrian Lloyd) for Hania. The ship anchored in Syra all day and started for Hania at 10.30 p.m.–making a 15-16 hour voyage. Crete in sight at 1 p.m. 'Persia' pitched, but rolled on a little. At 5 p.m. entered the port of Hania. But the beautiful approach of the island, of course, I did not see, as it was hidden in clouds, and latterly heavy rain. Port is very picturesque, Pasha's Palace etc etc but, the boats, and the eleven objects got on shore. No trouble with luggage etc. But the hotel (Constantinople) what a place!!'

Edward Lear, a household name with us since childhood with his limericks and poetry:

'The Owl looked up at the stars above
And sang to a small guitar
O lovely Pussy, O Pussy my love
What a beautiful Pussy you are...'

Alas, Edward Lear was not happy in his two months in Crete. April was still early in the season and the rain often prevented him from drawing out of doors. Within its Venetian walls, Hania was crowded with people from many lands, plus cats, dogs and rats. The Cretans in their baggy trousers were scarce, as most lived out in the country. The town was overrun with Turkish soldiers, Albanians, Egyptians, Armenians, Jews and Gypsies. Many leprosy victims walked the streets and the town was generally run down and filthy.

The Consuls of the Great Powers had their establishments outside Hania's town gates, a kilometre away in Halepa. This is where Edward Lear found more congenial company and lodgings with the British Consul (Mr Hay) and his family. The Pasha at that time was Ismail Pasha, whom Edward Lear visited in the Serai (Palace).

It could have been that James Lindsay had, by 1869, the same travelling experience as the Pasha. I read that from 1868-1877 Raouf Pasha travelled between Crete and Constantinople three times. The Pashas were often recalled to Turkey when troubles arose and then returned to Crete.

Raouf Pasha was popular and a close friend of both the British and French Consuls. Why not James Lindsay as well? I like to think of their travelling from Constantinople together on the Lloyd. In 1852 Veli Pasha had built a mansion in Halepa, which was to become the Lindsays' first home in Crete and an important location for my family.

So, if all went as I visualise it did, Raouf Pasha rode in a carriage with James and Betsy Lindsay, a cart with their belongings following behind: the wooden trunk, hatboxes and a lot of other household goods, the soup tureen and opaline glass lamp, which I look up and see as I write (I have always been told that it was brought from Constantinople). They passed through the gate of the walled town of Hania in to the open countryside, dotted with newly-built villas housing the Consulates, then along the coastline towards the east. With the White Mountains rising majestically to the south, they drove a kilometre to Halepa and up a small incline to a large mansion with a grand gate and pebbled courtyard (still lovely today), outhouses used as stables, wash house, coach house and the magnificent wrought-iron double staircase leading to the entrance hall of the mansion. It was described as 'Bridge House' in letters written from Granny to Eva many years later. There is a dark covered passage leading from one road to another, hence the name.

Raouf Pasha helped them settle with their servants and other necessities. Next morning, James Lindsay must have set out either by carriage towards town and then turned east to Suda or, as we did so often in our youth, crossed the neck of Suda on foot, though it is more than likely that Lindsay would have been on horseback. Once in Suda, he would have inspected what had been started at the Arsenal and what was still to be done.

I like to intersperse my narrative with present-day stories. A few years ago, I was in a shop in Hania and I was asked for the umpteenth time where I was from. I said I was Cretan but as usual I am pressed for more details because I have slight Scottish features. I replied I had a Scottish grandmother, but that wouldn't do, I had to say more. "How come"? (Cretans are curious people). I continued talking about my grandmother's uncle, James Lindsay, and the Arsenal at Suda. "Ah!", said the shopkeeper, "my grandfather worked as a builder with the Englishman Tselebi" (Turkish for Master). How vivid the whole picture is: the Cretan workman with a wheelbarrow of stones, Uncle Lindsay a Scotsman, not an Englishman, kindly yet firmly giving orders – and the shopkeeper remembering.

Mr Hay, the British Consul, left in 1865. The British Consul in 1869 was a man called Dickson, shortly to be followed by a man named Thomas Sandwith, who became a long-standing close friend of James Lindsay.

I must digress again! Although I am not writing history, just a memoir, I must give a short, precise picture of the politics at that time.

Greece and the islands had been under Turkish rule for 400 years. The date 1821 marks the great uprising on the mainland with Greeks fighting for their liberty and independence: 'Freedom from the Turkish yoke'! was the slogan. Also at that time, another Scotsman demonstrated an interest in and love for Greece: Lord Byron. Again, I hear Granny Jessie saying that at the age of 18, it was her knowledge of and respect for Byron that had influenced her decision to journey to Crete and live with her uncle and aunt. So, with the mainland liberated, the islands rose up at different points in time to shake off the Turkish yoke. That gave Crete the initiative for union with mainland Greece. However, the 'Great Powers' of the world were deeply involved in Greek politics, each one more interested in their own advantages than in the welfare of the island. Of the foreign powers, Britain was the most popular with the Cretans.

At this time, foreign powers were putting pressure on Constantinople to alleviate the condition of the Cretan people. Eventually the 'Organic Law' was drawn up in 1867, resulting in equal rights for both Christians and Turkish Muslims, with an equal representation in the administrative hierarchy. Although laid out on paper and agreed to by both parties under pressure, in reality the clauses of the declaration were far from satisfactory, firstly, because the clauses were signed under pressure and secondly, because the majority of Cretans were for the union of one great nation: Greece.

Just a fraction of the number of uprisings after 1821 were in 1841-1858 over the 'Organic Law', in 1878 and between 1895-1897, which was the last political episode in James Lindsay's life. Each uprising involved taking up arms and fighting from mountain strongholds. Women did their best from home and often participated in the protests. Crops were neglected, agriculture and livestock ruined. As each uprising failed, the Turkish rulers took revenge, with the result that many political refugees fled to the mainland and freedom.

It was only many years later, in 1913, that Crete joined Greece as one nation under the Cretan politician Eleftherios Venizelos. Sometimes I stand in awe of the way the Cretans survived and also kept their national identity, their culture, religion and particularly their character and their joy for life and freedom, during so many centuries of adversity.

What marked the Cretan character then reappears in recent times, most notably during WWII. 'Uprising' on Crete became such a national trait (much like the Scots and their history) that, barely armed, they rose to fight the Germans in 1941 in acts of bravery, that in retrospect helped the Allies win the war but brought such cruel reprisals by the Germans.

James Lindsay was to experience the later uprisings of 1866-1878 and 1895-1897. I remember Granny Jessie saying that when Uncle Lindsay first came to Crete he was very pro-Turkish. It was only years later, when he watched the cruelty and injustice imposed on the Cretan people, that he turned towards the land he had adopted with a full heart.

Chapter 4

Bridge House and Lindsay House

James Lindsay was not the first of his clan to set foot on the island of Crete. In 1356, the time of the Crusades, the Earl of March, George Dunbar, died in Crete. (*Scotland and Crusaders, 1095-1560*, p. 88). But, what seems more important is an item from the *Lives of the Lindsays* (vol.1, p. 73): 'In 1382 Sir Alexander Lindsay of Glenesk died on the island of Candia (old name for Crete) on his way to Jerusalem'. What did he die of? Wounded in chivalric games? An accident? Malaria? All records are lost in the mist of the island's past. And in 1869 another member of the clan was to come to Crete, to work, love and die here – James Lindsay.

Bridge House was a spacious mansion in Halepa, an affluent area on the outskirts of Hania. Large houses dotted the fields and gentle slopes, always with the sea to the north and the White Mountains to the south. Even after 150 years or more it seems to have retained some of the features of its former glory: gold leaf on the cornices and the central ceiling intact. I have only stood on the outside with my cousin Tricia, as we looked down on the pebble courtyard and thought of my mother and Tricia's father as children playing. It is strange that at this very point, when I am searching for the history of the house, it should be changing completely. New owners have bought the property and plan a full renovation.

It is now established that the Lindsays settled in to Bridge House. What we know about the house is that it was built by Veli Pasha in 1852 on the ruins of an old Venetian building. James Lindsay would have driven his carriage or rode a horse to Suda daily, whilst Betsy would have remained at home seeing to the servants and doing her needlework. I remember an octagonal table with four small drawers that was Betsy's embroidery table.

However, there would have been a language barrier for them within their new surroundings. James may have picked up a little Greek in Constantinople but he would have been speaking Turkish. As for Betsy – what did she know of the Greek language and the Cretan dialect?

We must not think of Hania as the last of the 'wild places'. Apart from the natural beauty of the island and the remarkable climate, there were many foreigners living in the town and its outskirts. The 'Great Powers' – England, France, Austria, Italy and Russia – all had their consulates in Halepa, where they lived with their families and maintained a busy social life. Edward Lear writes of the pleasant musical evenings spent with the British Consul Mr Hay and his wife and small daughter.

Betsy Lindsay (how little I know her), I hope, looked kindly on her new circumstances, the island and people. The servants would have been eager to please as Cretan women were, and are still, well known for their kindness, generosity, cultural background and skills in housekeeping, weaving, lace making and embroidery. Did they show her their weaving? Did she take an interest?

In 1872, when the Arsenal was more or less completed, the 'Grand Inauguration' took place, with many officials present, including the Sultan Abdul Aziz, who came over from Constantinople to attend. An old script records how the road from Hania to Suda (a distance of 3 miles) was spread with carpets in his honour. The principal personalities on that day were James and Betsy Lindsay, who sat at the Sultan's table. Was it there that the Lindsays felt the strong attraction to the peacefulness and beauty of Suda, and their hearts were won over to spend the rest of their lives there?

They bought a plot of land just opposite the Arsenal, on slightly raised ground, with Suda Bay below them, behind the house the hills rising to Malaxa and, further up, the magnificent White Mountains. Suda up until WWII was sparsely inhabited. Even as a child, 50 years after Lindsay House was built, I remember the peace and quiet of the place. We would take our evening walks towards the British Cemetery with the sun setting behind the town of Hania to the west. If the British fleet were anchored in the bay, we would watch the lowering of the flag and hear the sound of the Last Post, which still comes back to me when I listen to Beethoven's *Leonora*. Today there is very little left of the old Suda. Today it has become the commercial harbour of Hania with unattractive buildings, concrete, traffic congestion and noise. However, on the Suda road there are still a few eucalyptus trees, which were planted all those years ago by my grandfather, George Couryeraki.

Although the official inauguration of the Arsenal was in 1872, Lindsay was still employed by the Turkish Government until 1879 when he retired. The British Consul Dickson mentions that Lindsay was also responsible for the repairing of damaged ship engines and spoke very highly of him. I think Dickson replaced Sandwith for a short time, as Sandwith was British Consul from 1869-1881 and a close friend of Lindsay, so it must have been around 1874 that James and Betsy decided on a home in Suda. He was about forty-five years of age when he reached Crete, and both his salary and later his pension would be adequate for a good comfortable lifestyle.

Granny often described the building of Lindsay House when the foundation stone was laid, and a few sovereigns were placed on the foundation stone, as was the custom. When the walls went up and the workmen were ready to start on the roof, a cock was boiled and the workmen ate the broth in celebration.

On the ground floor there were three rooms and a large kitchen with two long narrow rooms: one used as a bathroom and the other a pantry. The pantry I remember well. Along the side wall ran a cupboard, which had fine wire-netting on the doors and shelves for foodstuff that needed airing. A few steps led down to the cellar; I suppose the demijohns of oil and wines were kept there. It was less in use as a cellar when I remember it, but a great number of magazines, books and newspapers were stacked down there, with a musty earthy smell. Crystalie and I, on our Sunday visits to Granny's around 1925-1933, delighted in rummaging in that cellar.

On Sundays we would start early from Bella Vista, either by carriage or car, and drive to Suda. Once we had said hello to Granny and left Mother helping with lunch, we would accompany our father and go down to the harbour, where a fisherman was waiting for us in our own rowing boat, named the *Iolanthe*. We girls loved rowing and we had learned how to keep the boat steady before dropping the line into the water. We all had our own fishing gear, string not nylon, wound round a square cork so that the hooks could be fastened when not in use. Oh dear, how well I remember the pull of the fish on the bait. The bait was shrimp, passed through a hook from head to tail. Our boatman, who probably had the use of the boat on weekdays, was a local man, half-Cretan, half-Turkish, who I think didn't think much of young girls mixing with fisherman's work. But my father, who may have wanted a son, always treated us close to his heart. His wife and three daughters were not treated as inferior, as was usually the case on an island so recently liberated from Turkish rule.

At midday we would return to Lindsay House where Granny and Mother would admire our catch and, with a lot of 'blether' over our fishing experience, we would sit down to our Sunday meal. When the meal was finished the adults would retire for a siesta, but Crystalie and I would rummage in the cellar below the pantry for something to read. Crystalie was a great reader; I was not, but I do remember a pamphlet on the Covenanters. The illustration on the front page was of a small boy, held by the scruff of the neck over a precipice. He was carrying a basket with provisions for the Covenanters. His captors were demanding to know where the Covenanters were hiding, but he was a brave lad; he'd rather face death than turn traitor! But sometimes I would just lie in a shady corner of the field below, among the tall grasses with the bees, insects and butterflies and daydream.

The days were long. We had all the time in the world, as the summer shades lengthened, to sit outside the great creaking gate where two large eucalyptus trees whispered in the breeze above two stone benches built on either side of the entrance. The end of a perfect day!

But let us return to the house. At the back of the hall, next to the kitchen, was the back door leading out to the pebbled courtyard. Running along one side of the house was the coach house, wash house and a two-roomed corner cottage for the staff, but at that time I remember it being used as our playroom. Inside the house, just opposite the kitchen, was the staircase leading upstairs. It was rather square, and on the first turn there was a very tall window, facing south, with a wide sill. On the sill was a large glass case. The story goes that a majestic cock in the hen-house grew so fierce that nobody, except James Lindsay, could go near him. The cock had to be put down, but was embalmed, put in a glass case and placed on the sill, where he remained for many years until the house was badly bombed by the Germans in 1942.

When I stayed at Lindsay House with Granny, the house was very different from what it had been like when first built and life was so very different too. I remember the house as being very empty, with wooden floors that creaked. Upstairs there were four large rooms and a balcony overlooking the bay.

Now that I am back in Crete, the warp threads of the loom on the large wooden cylinder of my life, are coming to an end and, as it slowly turns to let loose more threads, I am now weaving my story in so many colours and the shuttle moves back and forth.

The plain story of James Lindsay would have only taken a page to write, but the long story of all of us, connected and involved with Lindsay House and Suda, is, I think, worth weaving. Instead of writing a long 'dated' narrative, I will go on meandering as I remember my own experiences and those of others. There is a lot more to come, of pain and joy, of sunshine and shade. Now that I have made contact with many relatives who are involved in this story, I feel that I owe it to them to write of the past and the present.

Chapter 5

Two nieces come to Crete
and we meet a new member of the family

I'd like to say something again about the background of local history in the years 1874 and 1875. The Organic Law of 1867 was in force, but too often violated by the Turks. There were organized congresses but the Cretans of Hania were not allowed to send their own representatives and those chosen were from the pro-Turkish Cretans.

There were three kinds of local people: the Cretans, who always fought for liberty and the Orthodox Church; the Turks, fewer in number and mostly army; and the Turkish Cretans, who were Cretans turned Muslim, which many had done in order to increase their livelihoods and escape taxation. Such Cretans were usually despised and often their behaviour was fanatical.

I remember as a child hearing my Cretan grandmother say that some Turks were honest and good neighbours. During the long space of 400 years, or 270 years on Crete, there was bound to be some intercourse between the two cultures. However, in reality it was religion, Orthodox Christianity and Islam, that created the divide.

The main issue was that the Turks were the invaders and the Cretans wanted their land back. After 1821 came freedom on the mainland of Greece. It is known that Veli Pasha, who had built Bridge House in 1852, was married to a Cretan Christian woman and, when they returned to Constantinople, he built a small chapel for her in the Serai (Palace).

In the years around 1874 Crete experienced very harsh winters. Bridges to more remote villages were destroyed, and snow cut off any communication. Many children and livestock died, crops were ruined and some people left the island to earn their livelihood on the already-liberated mainland of Greece, where the first railways were being built. They sold their plots of land and left. I remember seeing a pile of old land deeds, some in Turkish some in Greek, for plots of land around Suda and Tsikalaria that belonged to James Lindsay.

James had already established himself in Lindsay House and become a landowner. As I said a little while back, James and Betsy had moved in to their spacious new home, built with every convenience and comfort of that time, but they were lonely. So, they decided that each would bring out an unmarried niece from Scotland to live with them and look after them in their old age.

The two young girls would also be company for each other. Betsy wrote to her niece Maggie Montgomery and although I know little of her life before Crete, in an early photograph, she is a neat young woman with a large brooch on the bodice of her dress. The brooch was a design of two Ms, one in Gothic and one in English, and has been in my possession since childhood, when Granny Jessie gave it to me; it has always been like a personal connection between Maggie and I. I was hoping to marry someone with the surname starting with 'M' but I never managed it. Recently

I gave it to Tricia's granddaughter, Maggie, who may do better than I in choosing a husband with a surname starting with 'M'!

How much do mementos mean to us? To me, they are like a 'string of pearls', linking me deeply to the person they belonged to: often it is the only link. What else do I know of Maggie Montgomery? Granny Jessie said that she had a wound on her foot that would not heal. Why she decided to come to Crete and spend her life close to her aunt Betsy, we do not know. She certainly figures prominently in the lives of the Lindsays in Suda, and later I will include her little narrative: 'A Scotchwoman's Experience in Crete'.

James Lindsay's niece Jessie, I know very well, because she is my own flesh and blood. James's brother William and his wife Jane Horn had six children. William was a house painter, and later a potato merchant; Jane his wife, an attractive young woman. There were three boys – Willie, George and Robert – and three girls – Jessie, Nellie and Jane. Willie was killed in WWI and his name is included in the list of war casualties at Edinburgh Castle; I am close to Isobel May, his granddaughter. Robert was a sleepwalker; and a story tells of how when he was a small boy, whilst getting out of bed, he stepped on an earthenware chamber pot, which broke cutting his foot and shortly afterwards he died of gangrene. While I write this, I can hear Granny's voice telling me the story, which means so much more to me than it could to you, dear reader, who is only getting the facts. Photographs I have been looking at since childhood, letters, some of which came more recently from 'Suda' in Wormit near Dundee, and the sound of my granny's voice – so musical! I still have her Contralto Certificate and I remember her Scottish accent that 55 years in Crete could not scare away.

Jessie, my granny, was the eldest of the girls. Nellie married someone called Blain and went to Canada. I remember a photo of her outside her log home in her furs, with snow around her. Granny kept up correspondence with her until her death. Her son Bill may have died in battle, but in which war I am unsure. The third daughter, Jane Nichol, had a family in Dundee but later, when she contracted TB, she was sent to recover with her sister Jessie in Crete, in a milder and sunnier climate. But sadly she died in Bridge House. Her headstone and granite cross, sent over later by her husband, mark her resting place in the cemetery of Hania.

When Jane Lindsay died, William didn't take long to find another wife to look after his family of small children. Jessie, who was only eight years younger than her stepmother, was unhappy at home. She left the family home and started a milliner's shop in Carnoustie. When her Uncle James wrote to ask her to come out to Crete, she was only too happy to comply. I remember her saying that Byron was her reason and inspiration to come to Greece. 'The Splendours of Greece' – she must have already read *Childe Harold* and was probably ready for the adventure.

I try to remember what Granny Jessie often related of that remote past. She crossed the Tay Bridge a little while before the 1879 disaster. And then did she travel with Maggie? By train or by ship? They must both have been exhausted by the time they reached the harbour of Hania, to be met by Uncle James and driven to Lindsay House. However, the house was spacious and peaceful and, I believe, their new life under blue skies and sunshine started well.

How strange everything must have been at the beginning: the language, the baggy trousers! There is a great deal of material in the blue or black felt baggy trousers, which are cut on the bias that forms a large amount of material gathered at the back, forming a lump of cloth between the legs behind the knees. When walking, the cloth sways from left to right like the pleated kilt. Jessie was curious about the style of the trousers and when she asked her uncle why there was so much fabric at the back, he told her that the Cretans had tails!

There was young company now in Lindsay House. There were outings in the surrounding countryside and other foreigners to share a social life. James Lindsay was a retired gent by now, in 1879, with land to his name; olive and orange groves and cottages that brought in rent.

There is a story, though disputed by some members of our family, but which I remember being told by my cousin Isobel, who in turn had been told by my mother. One day, in about 1883, at the age of fifty-nine, James Lindsay was riding out on his own visiting his fields, when he met a young woman from the neighbouring village of Tsikalaria. The young woman, Skevi, was the local schoolmistress, and probably a person James could talk to about cultural and worldly topics. Whether the relationship was a brief encounter or a more lasting affair we do not know, but a little girl was born. Her name was Evanthia, Eva. She grew up to be the joy of James's life and of the lives of all around her. But such joy has its penalty in pain. Eva was adopted and taken to Lindsay House by James Lindsay and her natural mother, Skevi, would have faced, among other things, the pain of being separated from her child. Thankfully, a document I have seen states that she later married and I hope she had her own family. However, in Lindsay House there must have been pain and embarrassment, which would gradually pass to make way for the joy and love that Eva was to bring to those in Suda and many others in her life. There is an old sepia photograph of James and Betsy sitting side by side on the covered balcony of the top floor of Lindsay House, Jessie and Maggie stand side by side on the lower terrace and, in the foreground, stands a little girl of four or five, Eva, in a white pinafore. The picture describes the scene at Lindsay House in about 1889.

There was also to be another crisis in the Lindsay household a little later. But just now I will follow the story of Eva Lindsay, mostly contained in our memory and in a few letters found in the musty leather satchel, which still lies in a drawer in the house named 'Suda' in Wormit, near Dundee. I must quote from one of these letters. Jessie writes to Eva, who is now married and settled in Dundee. It's a long and reminiscent letter informing her of the death of Maggie on Oct 24th 1917: *'when you were at the French School, and staying with me at the Bridge House in Halepa, I should say about 23 years ago'*. That would make Eva ten years old when she attended the French School.

The Catholic Nuns of St Joseph first came to Hania in 1852, where the Franciscan monks had already established a church and parish. At the beginning the nuns shared a building with the monks in the town centre and started a day school. There was a demand for learning the French language, especially from the numerous foreign residents of the town, many of whom were Catholic. Later, in 1892, the nuns moved to Halepa, bought land and built a school. It was there, while living with Jessie and quite close to Bridge House, that Eva attended the school and learnt French. At this time Bridge House was in Jessie's possession and it will link up my story as I go along. The letter I am quoting from was written to congratulate Eva on her forthcoming marriage to George Lindsay of Dundee. Eva seems to have grown up in the care of Jessie and Maggie, as Jessie signs the letter, *'your foster mother'*. I hope Eva was happy as a young child and girl when she moved in the society of her father and his immediate family.

Eva was twenty-two in 1906 when she first set out for Scotland. The following years were spent training to be a nurse at the Simpson Memorial Hospital at Lauriston Place, Edinburgh, and then working as a nurse. A document signed by a colleague, C. Dewar, in 1912 certifies to her identity: adopted daughter of James Lindsay.

Eva also kept two letters, one written in English and the other in Greek, both dated 1913. The English letter, pleading with her and accusing her of having a heart of stone, is written by a young Cretan man called Dionysis. He was deeply in love with Eva and wanted her to come back to Crete and marry him. His sister writes a letter in Greek, pleading on behalf of her brother, telling Eva in no uncertain words that the long years and persistence of his devotion, on her brother's part, were proof of God's will that she yield and accept the proposal of marriage! How hard was it for Eva to make the decision she made? That she kept those letters means that Dionysis had a place in her heart. In 1918 though, she married her father's nephew George Lindsay, and Dionysis went to America to an unknown fate.

On Eva's announcement of her marriage to George, Jessie continues to write in her letter,

> *'To give you my best wishes in the steps you have taken, and do you know that it was Uncle's wish that you two should marry, as far back as when you were with me in Bridge House in Halepa?'*

Then, in 1914, a letter to Eva from George's sister Lotty states,

'I am so glad about your engagement to George, and not at all surprised, I have often thought about the possibility.'

And so in 1918 (when I was one year old in Manchester), Eva married George Lindsay. The physical ties with Crete were severed, but there would be many, many, letters.

I stop to ponder on letter writing, the first letter written, the first postage stamp. Letters in our lives are as important as food and clothing. The use of pen and ink to mark down our thoughts and feelings, letters from and to the front, letters from a mother to a child away from home. Bernard Shaw said that the greatest love stories in the world have been conducted through letter writing. Letters travelled for years between Scotland and Crete, alleviating pain, separation and the nostalgia felt away from home.

Eva and George lived in various places in Dundee and moved house as their family grew. Their three sons Bill, Nicol and Bruce, were born before they moved to 12 Hill Crescent in Wormit, a large end-terraced property with wonderful views over the Tay of Dundee, where their daughter, Nancy, was born. Once their children had all left home to start their own families, George and Eva, her health failing by this time, moved to a more manageable house, on the flat, in Newton Park (now called Kilmany Road), where they named their house 'Suda'. In both of the Wormit houses, George built Eva a greenhouse, where grapevines were planted to remind her of Crete.

Eva had a good and satisfying life. Her gentle, loving nature made her loved by all around her, her own family and the numerous Lindsay clan. But, there was always a secret corner of her being. A letter from Crete would arouse her childhood experiences. As she cradled her daughter in her arms, she would think back on her own mother, Skevi. She would think of the sunshine and the White Mountains of Crete. Her daughter Nancy, in a letter to me says,

> *'I always had the feeling that James Lindsay was my Grandfather, it's such a pity that my dear mother had to feel ashamed of the circumstances of her birth. She was such a lovely mum.'*

And recently Nancy wrote in more detail:

Dear Marie,

Thank you for your letter. I have given up trying to type letters to you on the computer as I typed a whole screen about my mother then touched the wrong key and lost the lot before I could print it off!

To tell you about my parents, they were the most loving couple I have ever known. I never heard a cross word between them. Mum did her nurse's training (in the same hospital as I did mine) in Dundee before they married. She didn't have an easy life, as my grandmother, Margaret Ann, went to live with them the day they got back from their Honeymoon and decided she was an invalid who couldn't do anything to help Mum. Anyway, Mum did enjoy life and was a wonderful mother to the four of us. My only wish is that she had told us more about Crete and taught us to speak Greek; she had become a real 'Scot' and a Lindsay.

During the War she was very stressed as Nicol and Bruce were in France. Bruce came back from Dunkirk and Nicol a week later. Bill was in the Merchant Navy and his ship was sunk, he was on an open boat for 28 days before making landfall. Mum used to listen to the news on the radio and I would look at her lovely face with tears running down her cheeks as she worried about her sons.

Mum loved her garden, even in the winter when she would climb through the snow to attend to it. She was great at making jam and blackcurrant jelly and her scones were superb, a very good housewife.

My grandmother died in the November and Mum had her first stroke in the May, only six months of being able to do anything she wanted without having to think of her mother-in-law.

There are so many memories of her. When I started my nursing training I had a very strict Ward Sister, who reduced me to tears over nothing one morning when I was meeting Mum in town for coffee. I saw her coming along the road, she saw my face and put her arms around me. When I told her what had happened and that I wanted to quit nursing, she said, "Nancy, no Lindsay ever gives in". I have remembered that all my life and it has helped me very many times. She died on the 16th January 1953 leaving Dad and her family completely bereft. She was a great Mum.

Love Nancy

Her three sons, Bill, Nicol and Bruce, grew up and had families of their own and they all have a share in this story. For the most part, though, they did not know of their connection to Crete. We have moved in to a new century, where attitudes have changed so much, and where the circumstances of Eva's birth would be considered a joy in life, and a drop of Cretan blood means the enrichment of our genetic width, height and depth. Nancy, so close to her mother, as she too became a nurse and knew the alleviation of human pain in sickness and healing, has her own story to tell – as we all do.

I ponder again on the old sepia photographs: Eva as a child in her white pinafore; Eva, a girl in the courtyard of Lindsay House with Jock the dog; Eva, posing at the photographer's studio, wearing an elaborate dress and long black lace mittens; Eva, in Wormit, out on the lawn, matronly now with her sons and daughter, happily smiling with Jessie beside her, on one of Jessie's rare visits to Scotland.

It was in 1953 that Eva died following a long and painful illness. Nancy, who was away from home when her mother died, returned to be with her father. After nearly forty years, George Lindsay had lost his life's companion.

Eva must have felt the longing for the land of her birth as she neared the end. In all those years she had never returned to Crete. Nor had she talked to her children of the distant island that had been her birthplace and home in her childhood. She told her husband that she wanted to be cremated, and her ashes returned to Suda Bay. Nancy and her father travelled to Crete, where my father was still living: my mother was in Athens. A rowing boat took Nancy, my father and George a little way off shore. There, the ashes of Eva, adopted daughter of James Lindsay, were scattered and slowly sank in to the peaceful waters of Suda Bay. She had finally returned.

Chapter 6

Jessie and George – Crete 1887

Now we come to the second crisis in Lindsay House. A crisis does not always mean something leading to a disaster; it only means taking decisions, which can lead to very good results, as in the case of Eva. It's a decision that can lead to the unforeseen future. As this crisis concerns me and mine directly, I want to be very careful how I relate the story of my grandmother's marriage to the handsome Cretan, George Couryeraki.

The Couryeraki family, of pure Cretan stock, came from a mountain village. Yianni Couryeraki, like all Cretans, was prepared at any moment to fight the Turkish invaders, and at one point had to flee the island to evade reprisals. He sailed to the Peloponnese, where he stayed for awhile in Nafplion, then the capital of liberated Greece, and where he found himself a wife called Penelope. I always imagine her as small and dainty, with a lot of lace on the bodice of her dress. She came from a well-to-do family and had trained as a schoolmistress. My great-grandfather and his new bride returned to Crete. He built a house in Tsikalaria, where Penelope may have taught at the local school.

At that time, and even more recently, women had to have dowries when they married. These dowries contained household linen, kitchen utensils and general household goods – how very different from the families of today. In those days, the moment a girl was born, her grandmother, her mother and later she herself, had to start preparing for marriage. In the villages it was all done on the loom: sheets, pillowslips, towels and nightgowns were all woven. In the town, whole rolls of linen or cotton material were cut down, stitched, embroidered and trimmed with lace. There were also dowries that were wasted when a girl never married. Her dowry would stay folded away in a wooden trunk, turning yellow, and always with the scent of eucalyptus cones to keep the moths away.

Penelope married her Cretan husband and came to Crete, bringing her silver spoons with the engraved consonants of her name (ΠΝ ΛΠ ΛΙΡΓΑΚΙ). A single spoon still exists in each of our homes. It is possible that Yianni was responsible for the upkeep of Lindsay's properties and, of course, his own property. Yianni and Penelope had two sons and a daughter – Mikali, George and Sofia. When Penelope was mentioned in years to come, it was always to praise her and, when her younger son George proved bright at school, she saw to it that he went to high school to prepare him for a better life.

In 1887 Mikali was involved in catering for the foreign fleets in Suda Bay. The family also possessed flocks of sheep and goats. There was a letter, now lost, from Eleftherios Venizelos (later to become Prime Minister of Greece), addressed to the two brothers, Mikali and George, asking for quite a large number of sheep to be slaughtered and prepared as food for the insurgents, camped in Prophet Elias who were defying the Turks in 1898. Another letter, sent from Therisso, again addressed to the two brothers, accompanied some documents: the minutes of the revolutionary congress held in Therisso, which had to be, so the letter said, secretly delivered at night to some address. Venizelos signs 'With *brotherly affection*'. It is also said that when Venizelos visited Suda, he would visit and have a meal with the Couryeraki family, always in the company of George.

Back to Penelope, my dainty great-grandmother, who came all the way from Nafplion (although her name ending in 'akis' denotes a Cretan origin), the schoolmistress who moved from the capital of liberated Greece, to come and live in a small village in Crete. It is said that people live on as long as we remember them; true, but what do we really know of them, of Penelope, of her silver spoons? I am just listing names and relationships, but what can I tell you about the real person, their joys and disappointments?

Penelope's eldest son, Mikali, followed in his father's footsteps, dedicated to the flocks and property and married a young woman named Irene. They had a large family, whose children are very dear to me, but who remember so little of their past. 'Yes', there was a large box of old letters, documents, photographs, but perhaps when the Panormitis explosion took place in 1972 in Suda, leaving the top floor of the house and roof in ruins, they may have lost the box or it was taken to a relative's house for safe-keeping and, maybe sometime later, burnt on a bonfire as a useless old relic. And so we burn our bridges and advance in life without our 'relics'. Of course, there is the theory that the past is past and we must look to the future, but when we grow old, and the future is nearing the end, we immediately turn to the past. The past means so much to me now, because the future does not belong to me, but the past does: this host of men, women, children and old folk that walked the lane, which is now a highway, who breathed the same air and watched the same landscape and sunset, who all felt at different times disappointment and love.

Penelope's younger son, George, was a bright loveable boy. He did well at school and, probably at his mother's instigation, attended high school. When he was about twenty-five he had a great desire to learn a foreign language. Suda then was very international, with the foreign warships anchored in the bay. It seems the only one who could teach him the rudiments of the English language was Lindsay's niece, Jessie. So, the two of them sat across from each other at a table, learning nouns and irregular verbs. Jessie looked into his dark eyes and, comely figure as he was and a number of years younger, he looked back into the smiling face of Lindsay's niece, a Scotswoman. The attraction was there on both sides. What English language exercises George learned I do not know, but they fell in love.

The sedate Maggie Montgomery was quite content to remain a spinster, looking after her aunt and uncle, but Jessie was of a different calibre. As a girl in Scotland she had been vivacious and her knowledge of English literature enabled her to quote from Shakespeare. How the sound of her voice comes back to me. 'Patience on a monument, smiling at grief', she whispered to me so many years later, as I stood at the foot of her bed of pain. There was little to relieve her bone cancer in 1934. When she smiled at me, perhaps that love and bond between us was helping her bear the pain.

So, at the age of thirty-three, she fell deeply in love with George Couryeraki. Passionately in love, she was blinded to everything else. The 'unvoiced' agreement with her uncle – that she had come out to Crete for the sole purpose of caring for her uncle and aunt with no intention of ever marrying – was all erased from her mind. She wanted to marry her handsome Cretan beau. Did it surprise her that her uncle burst into a fury when she told him? Did she expect it? How am I to relate that moment in the life of Uncle Lindsay and his niece? The stubborn Scot, whose original plan was being questioned; did he not realize that his niece was still a young and vivacious woman looking out for a life of her own? In his fury, he packed her off back to Scotland, in the hope that she would change her mind – little did he know Jessie Lindsay!

It is from that time we have a lovely sepia photograph of Jessie in Dundee, surrounded by all her nieces and nephews, the boys and girls of her brothers George and Willie and her sister Jane.

But, my granny was a romantic at heart, even before she came to live in Crete, there were young men falling in love with her, such as Alan, who eventually went off to China as a missionary. I don't know how long she stayed in Scotland but eventually the power of love brought her back to Crete, determined to marry George. How deep the rift was with her uncle is a matter of conjecture. Granny always said that her uncle disinherited her. There was another story of Maggie taking Jessie's two children, Nellie and Jim, to see their great-uncle and great-aunt in Suda and Lindsay saying, "Take those brats away". Had he become a cantankerous old man?

A closer view of the matter made me think differently. He certainly never gave his consent to their marriage and very likely did not attend the wedding, as it would have taken place in the Couryeraki family home. We have proof of his desire to force Jessie into spinsterhood, which also suggests his belief that she may at some stage possibly marry, by what he wrote prior to Jessie meeting George, in his last will and testament:

'I direct my Trustees of my said niece Jessie Elder Lindsay, if then alive and has never been married, to allow her the free life rent, use and enjoyment of my heritage property in Ann Street, Dundee, but

that only so long as she shall remain unmarried and upon her death or marriage or in the event of her having predeceased or being married before this trust purpose in her favour would have come in to operation then I direct my trustees to convey over the said property in Ann Street absolutely to the said Evanthia my adopted daughter if then alive and whether she has married or not...'

The above will and testimony was sent to Eva when she reached the age of twenty-one in 1904.

George Couryeraki was handsome and a gentleman, and now he knew a little English, too, but he doesn't seem to have had a career: what did he do for a living? He would soon be starting a family, but on what financial basis? The Couryeraki family property would provide them with oil and wine, vegetables and fresh fruit, but was being in love enough?

The newly married couple moved in to Bridge House in Halepa, still leased by James Lindsay, and a period must have followed when Lindsay and Jessie were not on speaking terms, but blood is thicker than water. Eventually, it seems that all was well between them and Jessie was once again close to her uncle and aunt. There is an old sepia photograph of the elderly Uncle Lindsay looking down at Jim Couryeraki with an affectionate smile. (By then the family had dropped the 'aki' from his name and so I will refer to them from here on as Couryer.)

Jessie and George had two children: Nellie, who was born in 1892 and Jim in 1894. Two more babies followed, Manoli and Gemma, who both died in infancy. Their marriage began as a happy one, although there must have been vast cultural differences; Jessie, a young Scotswoman, well educated in the arts and society, and George, a Cretan Venizelist, passionate about politics which, at that time and even today, involves endless patriotic discussions. For Cretans it also means a rich spread of victuals and the consumption of a lot of wine and tsikoudia! From one account I have read, Venizelos would often visit the Couryeraki household when visiting Suda, and George was always there to greet him.

To make a living, George may have started as junior clerk at the Suda municipality, as later, when the municipality of Suda and Akrotiri were joined, he was elected Mayor. That must have been an affluent time for Jessie and her growing family, but I don't think that lasted long, and again there would be financial difficulties. Much later George got a job as a customs officer, which I imagine must have relieved matters.

The Couryers lived on in Bridge House. It must have been painful when two little babies had died, and no more came after that. Eva, as we know, lived with Jessie in Halepa and attended the French Convent School. It is at this time that we also get the first glimpse of religion in Jessie's life. A booklet on the Evangelical Church History in Hania, which seems to have been started by the British Bible Society, mentions the names of Thomson and Bruce as the inaugurators in 1887-1896, and that meetings were held at the house of someone in Hania called Theodore Mikailides. Sunday meetings were attended by James Lindsay and Jessie – also we are told of meetings taking place in Lindsay House and that members of the Evangelical community were invited to Easter festivities. There is also mention of Sunday school being held there at the Lindsays. We know that Sandwith, the British Consul between 1869-1889, joined in religious activities. I don't know when Mrs Watson, a missionary, came to Crete, I only know she left in 1910. From what I can gather, she lived with Jessie in Bridge House and from 1905 in Lindsay House. I believe it must have been Mrs Watson who fired Jessie with Christian zeal, which was so unsuited to her marital status. The Evangelical Church was built much later, and Jessie is mentioned as one of the founders.

I have to continue weaving the pattern of light and shade that gave some meaning to their life together. Today, when more than ever mixed marriages are the norm, origin still interests people. Some take it in their stride and others search for deeper meaning. There is a Greek saying: 'Wear a shoe from your own land, even if it is patched'. What made George Couryer marry Jessie? Her light-hearted smiling ways? What made Jessie marry George? His loveable handsome self!

In this narrative it is not necessary that I delve into their private lives. These two people, Jessie and George, are both dear to me. I, of course, blame the advent of Mrs Watson for the breach in their marriage. Religion can be wholesome if it is kept in the spiritual and celestial plane. Narrow-mindedness, bias and bigotry can be destructive and limiting.

I will just mention two little incidents, of which I was witness, in much later years. Mother was sitting by a window in Bella Vista, on a Sunday morning trimming her fingernails, when Granny Jessie came in making a fuss that my mother was working on the Sabbath. And again at Bella Vista when my father wanted his Sunday dinner to consist of roast beef and potatoes and Granny Jessie tried to lay down the law for a cold meal prepared the day before – so that there was no work done on the Sabbath. So, Granny Jessie, who was always smiling, being affectionate, quoting Shakespeare and singing her Scottish songs, had slowly become a biased narrow-minded religious convert.

So the rift between husband and wife was by then becoming more apparent at Lindsay House. Grandfather George wanted a table overflowing with food and drink for his friends and relatives, prepared by his wife, while Mrs Watson and Jessie were otherwise occupied holding a prayer meeting with hymn singing in the room above. When Jessie married, her brother sent her a lovely rosewood harmonium, so she could play her Scottish tunes and sing. But now it was only hymns she played. How often I have played on that harmonium!

George and Jessie were becoming worlds apart, each with his and her own interests. I have a small insight into the separate lives they were living in a letter from George Lindsay in Dundee to Jessie, where he states that he is very sorry to learn that George Couryer had to leave his house and go in to hiding because of a political situation. Was his life threatened by the Royalist faction? Could that be the reason that his son, Jim, had to be sent away to Scotland at such an early age?

I must not judge my grandparents, they may have always retained a deep love and respect for each other. But we have to remember the ancient Greek saying – 'Nothing in excess', and my granny's religious fervour was in excess. I know so little of my grandfather George; he died when I was nine or ten years old.

There is one last insight to what I have just said. Grandfather died from a wound to the back of his head, when he fell backwards at a merry outdoor gathering, enjoying life with his buddies. In hospital, during those last lingering days, he wanted no one but his wife at his bedside – Jessie and George at that last hour recaptured the affection of earlier years, the affection that was rightfully theirs. It was circumstances and influences that had caused them to drift apart. The pity was the inevitable trauma little Nellie and young Jim went through. I want to believe that time heals such experiences in life.

Chapter 7

End of the 19th Century – Crete

By the end of the 19th century there were many changes in the Lindsay household. A young girl, Eva, and two young children running in and out of the old spacious houses in Suda and Halepa, playing in the courtyards and the gardens of both homes. New life surrounded the old Lindsay couple. James, a retired pensioner, was still active; as the Consul Dickson says, James Lindsay was still responsible for repairs of ships anchored in Suda. He was also a landowner and the owner of a row of small cottages bordering Lindsay House and a row of small buildings closer to the sea front. One of the properties by the sea front was the 'Tea Room' for Naval Officers when ships were anchored in the bay.

Lindsay's friendship with the British Consul, Thomas Sandwith, must have given them mutual pleasure. The two men would meet and talk in their own language and discuss the continual conflict in local politics. Thomas Sandwith we remember as a great collector of Cretan handicrafts: lace, woven materials and embroidery. Many village women would knock on his door and bring items from their lovely dowries to sell for a little cash to buy provisions when times were hard. He knew little about a collector's business, but he knew there was value in these beautiful hand- or loom-made articles. Every item was labelled and noted down. What he gave in return was a little cash. There is never any mention of Mrs Sandwith in connection with the large Sandwith collection, which is now housed in the Victoria and Albert Museum in London. I was recently given the book *Greek Lace in the Victoria and Albert Museum* and was surprised to see that Sandwith's daughter, Charlotte, was Mrs Boys Smith, Granny's lifelong correspondent. How well I remember her letters arriving in Crete and the joy Granny derived from that friendship.

Sandwith's home was in Halepa and the two families would visit each other, driving their carriages. The men would talk of the dire conditions of the island, while the women folk would have tea and freshly baked scones, exchange fashion reports and the latest news from Britain. Would they also take drives into the rural countryside on those long summer evenings?

Time passed in Suda and Halepa. Sandwith and Lindsay both held the welfare of the island in their hearts; more so Sandwith, who owing to his position as British Consul, took an active interest in the Council Agreement of Halepa, when pressure was laid on the Turkish government to respect the rights of the Christian population.

That long period in Lindsay House in Suda, at the end of the 19th century, would have slipped by unrecorded had it not been for Maggie Montgomery, who decided to put some letters she had written to a Minister in Scotland into book form, so that by selling the book a little cash could be raised to help some of the needy in Suda. The last copy of 'A Scotchwoman's Experiences in Crete' passed from Granny Jessie to Mother and then to me. Its faded green cover was proof that it had been read a lot. Alas, it is now lost, but I had made a copy of all but the last page or two, where it is stated that Uncle Lindsay's last wish was that Lindsay House should become a spiritual home for the faithful in Hania. I now take it up and re-read it. I had thought of just copying some extracts, but I think it should be printed in full at the end of this memoir. It is the only direct insight into the private lives of the Lindsays in Suda at a certain moment towards the end of their long life of thirty years on Crete.

Maggie Montgomery ends her narrative with the death of the old folk. Uncle Lindsay died in Lindsay House in 1899 at the age of seventy-five. Both Jessie and Maggie looked after him until the end. Only a year later his wife died, not in Suda but in Halepa. Why was Maggie unable to have her aging aunt in her own home? Maggie died sixteen years later.

Looking back I only wish I knew more about my ancestors. I can only stare at the sepia photos and ponder. Had James ever gone back to Scotland? If he had, there would have been some record. All we know is that later, in 1906, Maggie and Eva travelled to Scotland together, Maggie for a short visit and Eva for good. James Lindsay had lived a good life with his family and those around him. In addition to his friendship with Sandwith, there were many other friends he made in Suda: British naval officers, Greek and even Turkish, I should imagine. He was a man of substance, and a small incident came to my knowledge only recently of his skills in the upkeep of his land. One of Lindsay's orange groves was later sold to a local farmer, who told me that the irrigation system that Lindsay had installed nearly a hundred years ago was still in use.

James Lindsay and Betsy Bell were laid to rest in the British Cemetery in Suda. It was a lovely walk there from Lindsay House, about half an hour to the east of the town. One of our favourite walks to the cemetery was over a hillock of wild flowers. The cemetery was surrounded by a tall wall with a wrought-iron gate, which creaked on its hinges as we pushed it open. There were a number of cypress trees and low geranium bushes. The British Government paid for its upkeep for many years. One of the grandest and most ornate gravestones was that of James Lindsay and Betsy Bell. One of the other less conspicuous stones was Maggie Montgomery's. There are also graves for British and other nationalities: consuls, naval officers and war casualties. At one end there was a row of plain slabs, perhaps six or seven, belonging to some Russian sailors who had died during a drunken brawl in Suda. As we sat on a grave or wall, Granny Jessie and Mother would tell us these stories. How well I remember our walks there on long summer evenings when we young girls would recite Wordsworth's 'We are Seven'. Did I sometimes go there alone?

The years passed, the First and Second World Wars began and ended, wars that really brought damage to our lives. Connections and family history were brutally severed. We grew up, we lost touch. Perhaps now more than ever before people are searching for their pre-war roots, trying to remember the past, just as Roy and Eric Lindsay picked up that photograph they found in their grandmother's leather satchel, and came all the way to Crete to discover their 'namesake'.

After the last war, the old British cemetery was demolished and a cluster of houses was built on the site. The British War Cemetery was already taking shape, in a peaceful valley at the head of Suda Bay. We were all away from Crete then, but a friend of the family at the Arsenal notified those responsible for the Lindsay grave. The remains of the grave and one or two others from the old cemetery were transferred to the new graveyard.

I read somewhere that 'a story is a letter that the author writes to himself, to tell him things that he would be unable to discover otherwise'. I think that is what I am doing. Sometime before Prince George set foot on Crete (I may go into that intricate story later), and before the century ended, in 1897 the final Cretan uprising for independence and union with Greece took place. The heroes of the moment were the politician Eleftherios Venizelos and later the writer Nikos Kazantzakis. Sadly, Lindsay did not live to see peace and prosperity in Crete.

left: Our Home at Halepa: Bella Vista

below: Iolanthe and Crystalie in National Dress at Bella Vista

above: James and Betsy Bell's gravestone, Suda Cemetery

left: James and Betsy Lindsay

below: Helen Lindsay with her parents, Robert and Janet

above: Lindsay's potato store, Dundee

below: Portraits of Robert Lindsay and his wife, Janet Elder

William Lindsay

Jane Horn, wife of William Lindsay

Jessie Lindsay (my grandmother)

Maggie Montgomery, Hania

mes and Betsy Lindsay and Maggie
Montgomery

Thomas B Sandwith, aged 49 in 1880

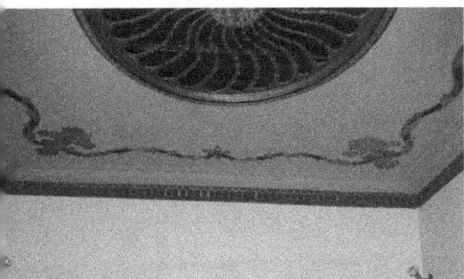

left & below: Interior and exterior
staircase of Bridge House

Lindsay House, 1875

LR: Crystalie, Marie, Iolanthe, Nellie and George Naxaki, Lindsay House, c. 193

above:
Lindsay House —
view from the east

left:
Lindsay House —
view from the south

below: Entrance to
the Great Arsenal,
Suda

Willie Lindsay and his sister
Jessie (my grandmother)

Jessie's brother, George Lindsay and
wife Jessie and family

Jane Lindsay

Nellie Lindsay (Blain) and son Bill in
Canada

Right:
Jane Lindsay's gravestone, Hania Cemetery

Below:
Willie Lindsay's daughter, Bella

Below right:
Willie Lindsay's daughter, Jean

above:
Maggie Montgomery, James Lindsay,
Betsy Lindsay, Eva and maid

right:
Eva, Jim and Nellie Couryer

left:
Granny Jessie, Eva a
George with Roy an
Eric Lindsay

top: Lindsay House — Maggie, Eva, Betsy, Jim and James Lindsay

above: Eva in Dundee 1947

right: Granny Jessie in Dundee with nieces and nephews

left:
Jessie and George Couryeraki with Nellie and Jim (my mother and uncle)

below left:
George Naxaki and Nellie Couryeraki on an outing

below:
Marie Naxai Karioti at James Lindsay's grave relocated to war cemetery in Suda

dding party for George and Nellie Naxaki

r family home, Manchester

her with Crystalie & Marie

left: Granny Jessie with uncle Jim in Dundee

below: Auntie Peggy and uncle Jim and daughters Tricia and Marion

bottom left: Simon Pryor

bottom right: Nancy Lindsay Payne

Chapter 8

Lindsay House and Revolution

In October 2005 Harry Fitton, aged five, sat down on the old stone steps and scratched his leg where nettles had stung him. He, his mother Sarah and his grandmother Marion had been trying to scramble over nettles and rubble from the back to the front of Lindsay House. I looked down at Harry and said, "This house was built by your great, great, great uncle". Harry looked up in perplexed disbelief. For him this 'great, great, great' was as far back as the story of the Minotaur he had been re-enacting a day before when he was coming down the road into the Sfakian village of Anopoli. For me, who was once again visiting old Lindsay House with relatives who had crossed the continent and sea for one more holiday in Crete, it was a moment of sentiment and memory. The grey walls guard their story and we all come close to listen.

The story of Lindsay House does not end with the passing of James and Betsy. The house was still in its prime. At the turn of the century, Maggie Montgomery was the only occupant. The engraving on the tombstone says that James

Lindsay died in 1899 in Suda Bay and Betsy Bell in Halepa in 1900. James died in Lindsay House, but Betsy died in Halepa under the care of Jessie. And then a few years later, in 1905, letters stop coming to Bridge House and from 1906 on letters are sent to Suda. It is hard to visualise what exactly happened at that period of time. Did they choose to live at Bridge House in Halepa because it was closer to the French Convent School both Eva and little Nellie attended, and also closer to Jim's school? I know that when Jim attended school in Hania he rode a horse there and back, but he was not a very studious pupil, and he would ride his horse far and wide instead of attending his class – at least so the story goes.

Eventually, Jessie and her family moved back to Lindsay House in Suda, to live with Maggie. Jessie still lived there after Maggie's death in 1917 and later shared our home at 'Bella Vista', until she died in 1935.

The end of the 19th century and beginning of the 20th was a very decisive period in the history of the island of Crete. In 1898 Prince George, brother of Constantine, King of the Hellenes, was appointed High Commissioner of Crete and disembarked at Suda.

The 'Great Powers' – Britain, France, Italy, Austria and Russia, whose role it was to guarantee the peaceful hand-over of Crete by the Turks and who, of course, have always taken it upon themselves to solve other people's problems – made the decision to appoint the Prince.

Prince George was the brother of the Princess of Wales who married 'Bertie' and later became Queen Alexandra, Victoria's daughter-in-law. Prince George was young and very handsome and, I am sure, started out with all good intentions: he was greeted with a warm welcome by the Cretan people. The first step was to shake off the Turkish yoke, and the union with Greece would follow. Everyone, of course, was not of the same opinion. Foreign countries were vying for supremacy in this part of the Mediterranean and Greece, not long rid of the Turkish occupiers, Greece was busy establishing rule on the mainland and not interested in problems with Crete. I believe that the Prince had the welfare of the island in his heart and, also, financial aid accompanied his appointment, so necessary to a poverty-stricken people. Many of the grand buildings still standing today date from the period the Prince spent in Crete and Hania, then the capital of the island.

We also have Maggie's account of a visit by the Princess of Wales to Lindsay House, to thank James Lindsay for his care of the people in his neighbourhood under persecution. However, Prince George was a foreigner to the Cretan people. Deep in their hearts, Cretan men and women are rebels and long years of slavery and suppression had forced them to continually fight for their independence.

Many rebelled against the rule of the Prince and it was at this time that the name of a young man was first heard, Eleftherios Venizelos. Born in the small village of Mournies a short distance from Hania, Venizelos had studied law in Athens and was now back in Hania, well versed in the high ideals and liberal philosophies of the West. His political views were broad and he could see further than the politicians who were wrangling over 'influences' and 'advantages'. He voiced out loud, 'Crete is part of Greece' and led a party against the Prince, with the immediate union with Mother Greece as the outcome. In 1905 he set up his revolutionary headquarters past the Gorge of Therisso, in the White Mountains. Not a shot was fired, but he let the world know that Crete wanted to be a part of Greece and not an island with a Foreign High Commissioner and he made his point. Foreign correspondents flocked to Crete and made their way up to Therisso to interview Venizelos. A lady correspondent, in a large hat and long skirt and practical British brogues, came too!!

I have a story to tell about young George Naxaki (my father) during the Therisso 'rebellion'. After finishing high school in Hania and a business academy in Athens, he was sent to the island of Naxos to study French with the Franciscan monks. On his return home, he found that his family were involved with Venizelos and the camp at Therisso and were responsible for the finances of the revolution. Venizelos had asked that a sum of money should be carried up to him to provide for his comrades. The government in Athens had sent a force of uncouth gendarmes to guard the pass to Therisso, and so keep the peace between the rebels and the Prince. How were my father and his brother to get past the Greek gendarmes? The brothers made a plan and set out together on horseback, my father pretending he was a French correspondent and making it imperative to interview Venizelos. All went well, my father aired his knowledge of French and Venizelos got his cash.

The Cretans rallied around Venizelos and the inexperienced and rather autocratic Prince fell from favour with the people. The Prince was eventually obliged to leave the island in secret in 1906. Meanwhile, Venizelos, the largest figure in contemporary Greek history (1864-1935), rose to be a Member of Parliament and Prime Minister. Politics is a favourite topic with Greeks. The last man in a Greek kafeneion today can discuss world affairs. Before and after the First World War, political passion was very high between Royalists and Venizelists. At one time Royalists all over Greece were encouraged to drop a stone in the village or town square against Venizelos. I suppose it was a sort of referendum and was called the 'anathema' (curse). It was there that Aristeide, my late husband, who was from a small village in Arcadia (Peloponnese), went to Tripoli to lay down his stone on the ever-rising pile. Later he would say it was the one act he was most ashamed of in his whole life.

The Couryeraki family Jessie had married into were all staunch Venizelists. Some of my Couryeraki relations believe that Jim was sent off to his Scottish relations in Dundee, at the tender age of fourteen, to be kept out of harm's way. It could be so, for no Cretan father would have allowed his only son to leave Crete if there were no good reason for doing so. But beyond that there is the hand of fate directing our lives. Uncle Jim made his home, his life and had his family away from Crete. And only once, a little before the Second World War in 1940, did he visit Crete and Greece for any length of time.

Crete is an island you can't write lightly about. The islanders' character, the island's history, culture and landscape are too outstanding. Isn't that exactly what links Scotland and Crete so closely together?

Chapter 9

A new member to the family –
my final chapter

It is now 1906. Granny Jessie and her family are all back in Lindsay House. Jessie would be aged fifty and Grandpa some years younger; Nellie was fourteen and Jim twelve. I try to picture the family in Lindsay House at about this time. The four bedrooms upstairs would belong to Maggie, Granny and Grandpa, Eva and Nellie, and Jim. Or perhaps, Maggie with her handicapped foot would be more comfortable downstairs, where there were three rooms, a bathroom, storeroom and large kitchen. (How familiar the whole house is to me.)

Eva was twenty-two and about to leave for Scotland. James Lindsay had been very precise in his will. If Jessie were to marry, she would forfeit any inheritance. And she did marry, God bless her: where should I be if she hadn't? So Eva went to Scotland, a supposedly well-off heiress, for all the Dundee property was left to her. The property in Suda all belonged to James's wife Betsy. After Betsy's death, so soon after his, Maggie, her niece, had a right to it all. Lindsay House was full of chatter again. Granny and

Maggie were like sisters and the three young ones attended primary school and also the nuns' Convent for both Eva and Nellie. And Grandpa George? A staunch Venizelist, at loggerheads with the Royalist party, but to his family a father and husband. I wish I had known him better. Granny Jessie at that period was wrapped up in religion. The small gospel community of Hania was doing well. Mrs Watson, the missionary, had arrived in Hania. She left in 1910, so I presume she was there some time before and, of course, living with the family at Lindsay House.

Even though Lindsay House was large, with space for all, there were separate 'factions'. Mrs Watson, Granny and Maggie were concerned with the salvation of the souls of the Cretans with prayer meetings and hymns. George Couryeraki on the other hand, in the same house, was upholding his political party views and taking an interest in local welfare, as (here again I have been unable to get a date) he was appointed the Mayor of Suda and Akrotiri.

Suda, at that time, was pestered with swamps that bred mosquitoes carrying malaria. It was Grandpa George, who as mayor, imported eucalyptus trees to absorb the damp of the soil underground, which helped to reduce the number of malaria mosquitoes in the area. However, many years later, in 1922, when I arrived from Manchester and we were staying with Granny Jessie in Suda, I contracted malaria and was rushed many miles away to Kolimbari, for a change of air and to recover. I was given quinine – not the sugar-coated pills of today, but bitter powder to swallow. Even at this distance, I still feel sorry for myself!

As a child, I would absorb everything I overheard, sometimes when I wasn't supposed to, and had my own feelings about my grandparents' life together. My memory of Grandpa is very vague, but I remember one time particularly, when we visited Lindsay House on a Sunday morning and were ushered in to a room (my sister Crystalie and I), where Grandpa sat in his armchair. We approached and were told by Mother to kiss his hand. (His hand had half a finger missing due to an accident with the reins of a horse. Granny rushed him to the British naval hospital ship in Suda, where his finger was amputated.) That was the only contact I remember.

By 1908 Eva and then Jim had left for Scotland. It was then that Maggie, travelling with Eva, visited Scotland for the one and only visit back to her native land. Jim had to travel alone in the care of a Welsh couple and the story goes that the couple took such a liking to him they wanted to adopt him! Nellie stayed in Crete, close to her mother and under the influence of Mrs Watson, who taught her the essence of the English language.

In 1910 there was another incident in the household. One day Grandpa arrived home with a small bundle in his arms, a baby boy. On his shirt was pinned a note: 'My name is Anastasis'. Here is Granny's statement of the finding of 'Archibald Lindsay Couryer', written in 1928;

> *'He was found in a field on the roadside in Suda, Crete on the 28th April 1910 – unwashed, a few hours after his birth. He fell into my hands the same day, and was brought up as our own child till he was eleven years old, when he was taken to Scotland and placed in the Quarriers' Homes, where he remained for over three years. Neither his nationality, nor his parentage was ever found out, though many enquiries were made. He was found at the time when the International Fleet was occupying Suda Bay, which lasted for years.'*

Archie brought little joy to the Couryer household. He was a strange and very naughty little boy. Nellie had to convey him for breast-feeding along a back street in Suda, two or three times a day. People would whistle: 'Is that your baby?' That was enough to turn any young girl against him. As Archie grew older, he was wild and undisciplined. One day he was playing with a box of matches and set his shirt on fire. Granny rushed him on board the British hospital ship, where skin from her body was grafted onto the wounded area. That wound gave him power. When he wanted something done he would scratch the wound and make it bleed. Granny loved the boy and I remember him well. I was attracted to him because he was naughty. He was with me in Kolimbari when I was recovering from malaria. We had a tent on the beach and Archie climbed to the peak and rolled down. I thought it clever and admirable, but my father gave him a spanking.

Later, Granny took Archie to an orphanage in Scotland. Even there he was problematic, he ran away more than once. Eventually he found shelter with Lillian Lindsay (great-grandpa's second wife), who took him in and helped him change his name from Couryer to Lindsay. He then sailed to Australia. Granny Jessie would await his letters with anxiety. We know he met and married a girl called June and sent a photo of her, which I remember well. We also know that he was good at carpentry and sent Granny Jessie a little wooden table and chair, for a dolls' house. Before Granny died, she had asked my father to send Archie a sum of money. Archie wrote to say he had received it but that was the last we ever heard of him. Somewhere in Australia his family are still living. How much were they told of Suda and Lindsay House?

Nellie was growing in to a lovely young girl, tall, slim, with thick brown hair worn in a long pigtail, which Uncle

Jim used to pull. They were very close and it must have hurt Nellie a lot when Jim was sent to Scotland. Still, she had her English lessons with Mrs Watson, French and piano lessons at the nuns' Convent in Halepa, tennis, books to read and embroidery to stitch and, from what I can gather, many admirers! Granny Jessie always wanted her to wear white, which set off her dark hair and blue eyes. However, as far as I have been told her relationship with her father was strained.

At this time there was the return of a young man named George Naxaki, who by then had left Crete for Manchester and gone in to the Ractivan cloth business. His father (my Grandfather Naxaki) was a cloth merchant in Hania, who died relatively young, leaving his sons to carry on the business, importing cabot and linen from Manchester. The young George returned from Athens and Naxos with a good education in Greek and French. His older brother was making plans to expand the business and was surprised, shocked and in full disagreement, when George set his mind on going to the Ractivans in Manchester, so that he could provide the shop in Hania with merchandise of his own choice. George sailed from Hania without his brother's approval, but eventually, with George in Manchester, the business flourished.

It wasn't so much the business that concerned George, but the spreading of his wings and experiencing a different European culture, where he had access to music, art and literature for which Manchester was famous, with the Hallé Orchestra and so much more. There was a large Greek community in Manchester and the Ractivan family were very good to him. George was at work during the day sending bales of fabric to Hania. He attended English classes in the evening and was generally becoming a real cosmopolitan.

Politics on the old continent were always troubled and Greece was involved in the Balkan wars. The young George Naxaki had already spent six years in Manchester and he and some fellow Greeks, bursting with patriotism, wrote to Venizelos, then the Prime Minister of Greece, offering their services in the Greek army. Venizelos welcomed them to Athens but only gave George a job in an office. That was not good enough for the young partisan and eventually he was allowed to join the fighting in the north of Greece. He was wounded in the leg and spent some time in hospital, after which he was sent back home to his mother's to fully recover.

On a bright windy day the young George Naxaki and his friend were riding their horses along the eucalyptus route to Suda, when a lovely apparition appeared before them – Nellie, a young girl of eighteen, dressed in white, with her long hair loose down to her waist. She and her friend Matilde were carrying between them a kite. The young George doffs his hat, the young Nellie Couryeraki looks the other way. When they passed, George told his friend, 'That lovely girl is to become my wife'. Next day he picked a rose from his mother's garden and set out again along the same route. The horses and riders were seen in the distance, and as they approached, he again doffed his hat and dropped the rose at my mother's feet, then rode on. On his return, the rose was still lying on the ground, making him even more determined to woo his belle. He made enquiries and wrote a letter to Granny, asking for an appointment to meet the young Nellie. When a time was arranged, he set off for Lindsay House, telling his mother that he was going in search of a wife. 'With my blessing', replied his mother.

However, this first visit to Lindsay House was dominated by the presence of Granny Jessie, who was delighted to meet someone who spoke English. George was immediately engaged in an English conversation with Granny and they talked of George's experiences in Manchester: even when Nellie came in to the room with the traditional spoonful of jam and a glass of cold water, they did not even look up for an introduction. But that was not to deter them: the young ones had exchanged glances and Granny gave George a copy of the English New Testament before he left!

Many, many visits followed. Now it was George and Nellie who spent time together. Young Nellie had a lump of sugar in her pocket for the horse and they would go out walking or, if George came in his carriage, driving together. I have another lovely sepia photograph of the two of them driving in a carriage along the Suda Road.

The Balkan war was over. Young George Naxaki got his medals and he was ready to go back to his business in Manchester, no longer a Ractivan employee but with a business of his own. Before he left, the wedding date was fixed. He would be back in one year to claim his bride. There was a packet of letters, tied with a blue ribbon, I remember in Bella Vista. Years later, Mother said she had destroyed them. When Mother died, we found the packet, still tied in the faded blue ribbon but only the envelopes were there.

Now began the bustling, stitching and preparation of the dowry. Irish linen, brought from the Naxaki shop in Hania, was cut to make into sheets and pillowslips, nightgowns and table linen, to which were added buttons and buttonholes, lace edging, etc, etc. Everyone thought they had a whole year to work on the dowry. Six months later, my father wrote to say he was returning earlier than planned – a year was too long to be apart! Everything now had to be packed in a hurry. Mother snatched a piece of linen, only half stitched, from Matilde's hands, which never got finished. The wedding took place in Lindsay House. I have a square of taffeta, pale blue with the letter 'E' for Eleni, my mother's name, stencilled in gold on one corner, a 'bonbonniere', for the sugared almonds offered at Greek weddings. I have another sepia photograph, taken a little after the wedding: Maggie, Archie, Matilde and my two grandmothers are there. The two missing are Eva and Uncle Jim. It is a lovely photograph: my mother, close to my father, but clinging with one hand to the toe of her shoe!

The young married couple went back to Manchester. They spent the first night at a hotel and next day George told Nellie that he had the key to a house, and if she took a broom and a shovel she could start cleaning it. They walked to Stoney Gate, Broughton Park and George turned the key.

Together they entered a beautiful furnished home: a rosewood piano, pre-Raphaelite prints on the walls, everything in my father's good taste. My mother had to learn early in her married life that my father was very good at practical jokes, but he was also a warm loving husband who set her on a pedestal, where she felt secure for the rest of her life.

We all know life is not a bed of roses. It has always been in my nature to look at the good side of things. Now, as an elderly lady, I want nothing to spoil the loving memories of all those people in the sepia photographs, and the impression of their lives and the love that marks them all for me now.

A fascinating stroke of luck

Simon Pryor

I, Simon James Pryor, first set foot on Crete on Friday, 20th April 2007. A short taxi ride from Hania airport later I was wandering through the old town in the early hours before tourists wake. The emotional impact of just the drive in to town and the short walk around the ancient city, about which I knew nothing, was enormous. Before meeting Marie Karioti, before learning anything about the land upon which I was standing, I found myself moved by an unsought but quite palpable sense of belonging. I sent a very simple text message to my wife, Judith Cooke: "Arrived, Paradise."

I began with the unfolding, ever-developing story of the Lindsays of Dundee and their associated families (including, by now, Cook-Pryor of Brunswick, Australia), their place, lives and roles in Crete and the nature and history of the landscape. This first task, I have concluded, will probably never be completed: the story is too rich, too thick as Clifford Getz would say, to ever be something that I and my immediate family could ever hope to fully comprehend.

A lot had happened before I was to visit Marie Karioti that April of 2007. It was a story of an adoptee in search of a mother and finding, unintentionally but gloriously fortuitously, Nancy Lindsay Payne and a welcoming extended family. It involved discovering an adopted heritage and exploring the possibilities of a new-found Dundonian heritage. It was a lesson in patience and understanding that it was entirely appropriate that members of the family associated with an Irish/Australian father were not willing, as yet, to explore the meaning of the change brought to their family story by a liaison on a ship between Naples and Southampton in late 1954. It was a story that brought out the impact one adoption of a tiny baby boy could have on the lives of so many. Indeed it was a story where adoption appeared to be a predominant theme, with my natural grandmother being born Evanthea Themaki in the Cretan village of Tsikalaria and then adopted as Eva Lindsay. But, most importantly, it is overall a story of welcome.

And so these 'Cretan cousins' met: Marie Karioti and Simon Pryor. "Ahh, sit you down", said an entirely Cretan woman to her Australian relative in a soft Scottish accent. I laughed with delight at the unexpected, yet with hindsight, quite obvious fact that Marie Karioti's Lindsay clan heritage would mean that she would learn from her family to speak Scottish English.

Since then, over the space of four years we have spent many days together experiencing the wonderful Cretan terrain, food, wine, finger lace, history and, of course, stories and friends. It is this relationship that has shaped much of my quite visceral sense of connection to Crete and its development, which will enrich immeasurably my daughters and their families as they fathom their individual ties to the land of their forebears.

One very important connection between the lands of Crete, Scotland, New Zealand and Australia came about in 2009, when, on Sunday the 14 June, my mother, Eva Margaret Nancy Payne passed away whilst Judith, Kathelleen and I were visiting Marie in Crete.

Nancy Payne's funeral was conducted by the Returned Services Association, for she was now a fallen soldier herself. But their ties to Crete are extraordinary, the Maori Regiment's role in Crete during WWII is legendary in both countries. They were moved by Nancy Payne's personal history and its connections to so many of their fallen comrades. Nancy Payne's sons, John and Ted, were struck by a richer understanding that their mother's Cretan heritage gave them of all that they knew and remembered of their lives with her in Africa and New Zealand. So much so, that they readily acceded to Nancy Payne's wishes that her ashes, like those of her mother, Eva Lindsay (Themaki) in 1954, be scattered in Suda Bay.

The more I learned about the Lindsays of Crete, the closer I became to my 'Cretan Cousins'. Marie's friends taught me about the history and landscape of the island and so the greater my conviction grew that this was where, as I started blurting out, 'my blood comes from'.

I was no longer a man in search of a past to lend meaning to an otherwise insignificant life. Instead, I was of Cretan origin and I could relax and let all else flow from that truth. It was as if my own 'thin' human construction; the way I actually saw colour, smelt smells, heard sounds, understood humour, felt weather on flesh, all made so much more sense once it was clear that this had all been born from the 'thick' cultural and genetic soup that is Crete.

Simon Pryor
21/5/2010

Letters

The account of Marion, Jessie Couryer's grand-daughter, of her father George James Lindsay Couryer and Nellie's brother, known as Jim.

'My father, George James Lindsay Couryer, was born on the 14th August 1894. As a small child and young boy, my father had a very happy childhood. He grew up with his sister Nellie, his mother Jessie, Aunt Maggie and Eva. However, he never talked of Eva when he told us stories of his childhood in Hania. I think she was quite a bit older and he probably did not understand the relationship; she may have been Uncle James Lindsay's daughter, nobody really knows. Jim's father did not appear to focus very much in his life, but I remember him telling me years later that he felt his father had been very misunderstood, perhaps because of cultural differences.

My father had his own horse, a boat, many toys and lots of Cretan cousins to play with. He had a very happy, carefree life. He played truant a lot when he should have been with the priests at school and was, I suppose, a little out of control, living with so many women and his father being absent from the house a lot.

His great-uncle, James Lindsay, did forgive Jessie and after the Turks left Crete it was fairly tranquil between them, at least for the immediate family. However, all this was to change in 1905, for Jim at least. He crated up and stored all his toys in large wooden boxes, obviously thinking he would be back before too long and life would return as it had been with his mother, father and sister.

He set off on a boat journey to Scotland, which would take seven to ten days, under the watchful eye of a Welsh family. He was very homesick and worried about going to live with people he knew little about and who he had never met. He may have been sent from Crete because of a vendetta, as his father was a Venizelist and these were very troubled times in Crete. The Cretans are well known for being a rather wild mountain people.

As mentioned before, on the boat Jim was befriended by a very nice Welsh couple, who did their best to comfort him. They became very fond of him and offered to write to his mother and adopt him. Needless to say, this offer was refused. The only person Jim knew when he arrived in Dundee was Eva, who had been sent there earlier to train as a nurse. But she was living in the nurses' home at Dundee Royal Infirmary.

His Uncle William, who he was going to live with, had in the meantime died. So he had to live with his mother's other brother George and his wife, Margaret. The cold climate and the very different, reserved lifestyle of his Scottish relatives did nothing to lessen his unhappiness. He was homesick for his family and the life he had left behind in Crete.

His mother and father were, of course, paying for him to live with his uncle and aunt. He was treated more as a servant than as a family member, having to clean shoes and wash windows etc on Saturdays. Although he was very unhappy, he did forge a close bond with his cousin George, who was older but helped him a lot in later years with his naturalisation papers, etc. He saw as much of Eva as was possible. She had also been treated rather unkindly by the Scottish relatives but in time she became the fiancée of cousin George and they eventually married. Her Cretan ancestry was always kept a secret as was my father's. It was regarded as something to be ashamed of and I am fairly sure their children were never told and I don't suppose they ever asked. We, as children, certainly never knew although we visited fairly regularly. All this family history has unfolded over a hundred years later. Eva's ashes were taken back to Crete after she died in the 1950s. Her mother's relatives, the Themaki's, however, were never traced.

My father attended Harris Academy until the age of 17. He then obtained an apprenticeship at Lowden Brothers, an electrical engineering firm and attended Dundee Technical College until he graduated as an electrical engineer. Electrical engineering was a highly sought-after occupation in those days with the fairly recent advent of electricity.

At the age of 21, assisted by his cousin George, he requested and was subsequently granted British citizenship. He then joined the army as an engineer, moving to many different Highland regiments, including the Black Watch, the Seaforth Highlanders, the Royal Engineers and the London Scottish. He was always hoping to be posted to France but, of course, engineers did not fight in the trenches. He did not know how lucky he was not to have experienced this. It was while in the army that he visited his sister Nellie, her husband George Naxaki and his two little nieces, Crystalie and Marie, in Manchester.

He was demobbed sometime in 1918, after the war had finished. His kilt was taken back to Crete and given to Nellie who had her dressmaker transform it into numerous dresses and coats for Crystalie, Marie and their sister Iolanthe.

Sometime after the war he set up in business in Dundee, but the venture was not successful. He then returned again to Crete, but his father had passed away.

He then joined a business called Whitehall Securities Limited in Athens, responsible for floodlighting the

Acropolis and installing electricity in the city. While working for them he was able to secure jobs for many young Cretan men. He was also, I believe, responsible for starting a football team, which was quite a novelty in those days.

It was in Athens in 1931 that he met my mother, Margaret Hannan, who was employed as a governess to a Greek family. In 1932 they married at the British Embassy in Athens. My brother James Lindsay Couryer was born later that year and taken to Crete to meet his grandmother, and his aunt, uncle and cousins. Unfortunately, there are very few mementos of his marriage as everything had to be left in Athens when the family returned to England in 1934. To the best of my knowledge, my father never saw my grandfather again once he had left Crete as a child. He was not present for his sister's wedding and only saw his mother once in all this time, when she returned to Scotland to bring Archie, an adopted foundling, to a Quarriers' orphanage. I think Granny probably meant well but was rather too old and unable to deal with small boys. She may also have missed her own son and did not have the necessary patience for poor Archie, who was by all accounts a difficult child.

My father was 38 years old when he married and had seen and done a lot by then, but had had a fairly traumatic life by anybody's standards.

I think, however, he was at his most contented when he married and had his three children, myself, my brother Lindsay and my sister, Patricia. We visited Eva and George in Dundee when we were children as they only lived 30 miles away, but I don't think they ever talked of their lives in Crete to each other or anyone else. It is now, so many years later, that we try to piece together all the pieces of the jigsaw.

On our side of the family there are six grandchildren and many great-grandchildren. I often wonder what he would have thought of all of them, not only Scots and Cretans but English, French, American and South African. What a wonderful league of nations.

Love Marion

The letters of Maggie Montgomery

The island of Crete measures 158 miles in length, from East to West, and its breadth varies from 8 to 40 miles. A great mountain barrier extends throughout its entire length, following the line of the South coast, and rising in two places to a height of 8,000 feet. The population, according to a census taken some fifteen years ago, numbered 280,000, three quarters of which is Christians. The main stock in undoubtedly Greek, and Greek is the language universally in use; but as regards the inhabitants of the low country, there has probably been a considerable intermixture with the different races who at various times had had supremacy on the island.

The people of the mountains, however, especially Sfakiots of the West, claim to be of pure Greek descent. Fine and independent-looking they are, but very lawless, not unlike our Highland clans as depicted in the novels of Scott. They have never been brought in to complete subjection to any of the races that have held sway on the island, and have been the backbone of every insurrection. In modern times the Venetian Dominion lasted 400 years, and that was followed by the Ottoman in the latter half of the 17th century.

One of the most obstinate defences recorded in history was that of Canea, then the capital of the island, the siege of which began in April 1667 and the town was not captured till the autumn of 1669. The Turks have ruled the country from that day to this, though happily the end of their domination is not far off. The most disastrous legacy of their rule is the presence of some 70,000 Moslems, the descendants of those Greeks who, at the time of the conquest, more than two hundred years ago, abandoned their faith to embrace that of Islam, and were awarded for their apostasy by the grant of the most fertile land on the island. Most of it is still in their possession, though much of it has been redeemed by the industrious and thrifty Christian peasantry.

Lindsay House, Suda.

A SCOTCHWOMAN'S EXPERIENCE IN CRETE
SUDA BAY, NEAR CANEA, CRETE

March 1906

My Dear friends,

Some years have elapsed since this little booklet was printed and many things have taken place in that time. Having been asked by a few friends in the navy and elsewhere, to have it reprinted, I thought in doing so I might add a little more, and thus increase the interest in Crete.

I had stated that European troops had come to the island, viz., British, French, Russian and Italian : they still occupy it.

Shortly after the British took possession of Canea, and while in the act of taking control of the Custom House, a premeditated massacre took place, which had a very sad ending and will not be easily forgotten. There were 14 British killed, also the British Consul, and a few wounded. Some cruel heart-rending murders were committed during that day : parents and children were separated one from the other.

But the Moslems soon found they had gone a step too far. British blood had been unjustly shed, and had to be avenged. This was quickly done by 17 of the Moslem ringleaders being hanged. But Admiral Noel was not satisfied until the troops left the island, which they did, in a very short time. The four powers promised the Sultan that he would still have a part in the affairs of the island.

The troops left much quieter than was expected. The next business was to choose a governor. Three were named. The one accepted was HRH Prince George of Greece, who received a hearty welcome as Lord High Commissioner of Crete, on the 22nd of December 1897. He promised much, and the people expected great things, but somehow they have been disappointed. Perhaps too much was looked for.

The Prince paid two visits to my uncle. The first was to thank him for the great help to the people in their time of trouble. On the next occasion he came with the Princess of Wales (now Queen of England) the Princess Victoria and her attendants. They were pleased to see the house and the fold which had sheltered so many in times of trouble and need.

The Princess told me that Prince George had given her the booklet to read. One part had made her very sad, that about the old man in the village who was forgotten when all the others fled, and on whom his neighbours had no mercy.

But all that is past and gone now, I should not like to go through the same again. The dear old couple has gone to their rest and reward. Uncle was the first to be called home. He died on the 17th of May 1899. Aunt died on the 8th February 1900. They had lived together for over fifty years, in death they were not long divided

They are laid in the British cemetery at Suda, where they so often walked. Many mourned their loss, and their memory is still cherished in the hearts of the people amongst whom they lived so long.

The house of refuge, as Lindsay House has often been called, is very dear to those of us who are still here. It is hallowed by many sweet and loving memories of the past.

A great deal has been said about annexing the island to Greece, but I am afraid that would not make things better. At present the representatives of the four powers are conferring to see what would be the best to do.

We are praying for wise decisions to be taken.

Ever sincerely yours
Maggie Montgomery

October 20th, 1896

Dear Sir,

You will see by the papers that Crete has for sometime been drifting in to a state of anarchy, murders being almost daily occurring. It was very rare indeed that anyone was punished for these murders, because when a Muslim killed a Christian he would immediately run off to where he knew there was a body of Moslem Police, who are always ready to protect the murderer of a hated assassin. He hears one of his relations has been killed, and his first thought is to take his revenge by killing a Moslem, whether he be a relation or not. 'Blood for blood' is his motto, and as a government won't extract the blood, he takes it himself. Of course he escapes to a hiding place which is known only to the Christian police. Thus the ball is kept rolling. Both sides know that there is no justice to be had from the so-called ministers of justice, so they take the law in to their own hands.

The Sultan kept sending one Pasha after another to put a stop to this state of things, but they couldn't do it. The people they employed to carry out their reforms were of course natives, and many had their own relatives to avenge, and if they hadn't they sympathised with those who had, and things went from bad to worse. The island was like a powder magazine, and an explosion might be expected wherever Christians and Moslems lived near each other.

Since the beginning of May the people in the village nearest to us, Tsikalaria, and the Christians living near us in Suda, begged my uncle to allow them to bring their boxes and household stuff to our house, as they were certain something dreadful was going to happen. Uncle could not find it in his heart to refuse them, as he quite shared their belief that evil days were coming. So day by day the people came down, bringing their bedding, kitchen utensils, and the trifles that go to make up the possessions of a Cretan peasant. Fortunately summer had set in, so there was little fear of rain, which seldom falls from the end of April till the middle of October. The refugees were quite content to bivouac in our garden, which as you know, is very large, and there is a vineyard besides, the whole surrounded with a solid stone wall.

So things went on until Sunday, 24th of May, our beloved Queen's birthday, when we hoisted the Union Jack in her honour, but the day had a sad ending for many a home. My uncle and aunt were resting after our early dinner, when a crowd of terrified men, women and children came running down from Tsikalaria, and they were joined by Christians from the houses near us. They clamoured for us to open the gate, and then they came streaming in, the men armed with guns, and men and women alike carrying such things as they had snatched up in their hurried flight. The news was of a massacre caused by the quarrel between a zappie (policeman) and the Russian Consul's cavas or bodyguards. The zappie was the first to fire his revolver, the ball grazing the cava's head; then the latter drew his sword, and ran the zappie through the body. When the Moslems saw one of their true believers dead, they rushed on the Christians, and before the authorities stopped the fray, 28 were killed and 11 wounded; though a few Moslems lost their lives in the struggle. Not a single European man-of-war was near the island, though the Consuls had been fully warned as to what might happen.

Well, to come back to our place. The first thing that my uncle did was to get the gate locked, and the refugees demanded their guns shouting, "If we are to die, let us die fighting". But uncle would not let any man fire on his premises unless someone was seen getting over the wall, which they did not dare to do. We then went to the balcony but could only see these five men slinking along as if they were looking for something. They soon saw their plan had failed and they slunk away. Thank God my uncle had the confidence and respect, for if not things would have had a different ending.

We have often thought over this incident since then, but we can come to no other conclusion that what we came to at first, that these five Cretan Moslems had been hired by those in authority to do their best to create panic among our refugees and tempt them to fire, and so to give them a pretext for firing on us with their big guns and blow our place to atoms.

Shortly after, a naval officer came to the gate with about twenty soldiers, and told my uncle that he had orders from his superiors to shoot English or any others who were disturbing the peace. Uncle told him where he would find the disturbers, meaning the five men that had been prowling round our premises, but of course he would never shoot a Moslem. Sometime after we saw the Governor-General's carriage drive in to the arsenal. What he said to the Commander we don't know, but reports said he was in a great state and told him it would have been a bad job for them had anything happened to the Englishman's consequences, and only regretted that they had not got their scheme carried out.

As soon as the Governor left, the Commander sent for my uncle. I may remark that this Commander was a notorious fanatic. He told my uncle that he had better communicate with his Consul and he would get the message conveyed, as we were cut off from all communication with Canea. Uncle hardly knew what to do, for we were doubtful the message would be sent. However he wrote to the Consul these words: 'Five p.m. Things at Suda very critical'. Within three hours five zappies were sent down from Canea following the Consul's representations to the Governor, and we had the zappies with us for nearly five months.

The next day, the 28th, the Consul himself came down, well guarded. We asked him if he did not think it was time we had British ships in Suda bay. He said he could not send for ships for everyone that asked, and that there was already one lying off Canea. I told him surely the British nation was rich enough to send more than one ship, as you know we were the only British-born subjects on the island. I added that if anything happened to us the blood would be on his hands. "No", he said, rubbing his hands, "I wash my hands clean, but I bring you the compliments of Captain Drury, of H.M.S. Hood, who says that if you are afraid, he will send round boats from Canea to take you on board". "Yes", I said, "but what about the refugees who are with us?". "Oh", he said, "we have nothing to do with that". "Well", I said "If that is all that you or the Captain can do for us, will you be kind enough to return the compliments to the Captain and tell him that if the worst comes to the worst, we can all perish together. We have given the poor shelter and we will not turn them out now, even at the cost of our lives, to be murdered as the Armenians were".

Very shortly after this, we had a British man-of-war at Suda bay and from that day to this we have seldom been without one. There is one thing I forgot to mention, which caused us much sorrow. A few days before the massacre, an old man who lived alone in the village of Tsikalaria, came down to our house and pleaded hard to be allowed to bring his bed to our garden, to live for a time as he was getting frightened. Uncle gave him a slap on the shoulder, and told him to keep his mind easy as there was no danger, and no one would harm an old man like him, but if later he saw real cause for alarm, he would be very welcome. But when the people fled from the village on the Sunday, the poor man was forgotten and I am sorry to say that his Moslem neighbours had no mercy on him, but cut him to pieces and threw him to the dogs.

I should like to give you the translation of an article that appears in the local paper of Canea, the first was printed after the disturbances of last May :

'The Very Reverend Archbishop Nikeforos of the diocese of Kydonia & Apokorona & Mr Lindsay are the greatest benefactors of the people residing in those districts. The Archbishop, with his kindly words of sympathy, exercised a powerful restraint on the Turks and saved the Christians from many a trial. Similarly the Briton whom everyone knows that lives in Suda, is the saviour of Suda and all the surrounding villages whose inhabitants took shelter in his house where the flag of England was hoisted. He is a true friend of liberty and no coward, because he disdained the offer that was made to him to take refuge with his family on board a warship, saying he would rather lose his life than abandon the poor people who came to him for protection.

Four hundred people had brought with them their furniture and livestock. He fed them for many days and at his request a man-of-war was anchored in Suda bay, whose presence put a stop to the evil works of the Turks who were busy burning and destroying.

This is a very long letter and I am afraid it will weary you reading it, but I could not help writing you some account of what we have been through.

Sincerely yours,
Maggie Montgomery

January 13th 1898

Dear Sir,

I gave an account, in a letter written more than a year ago of the massacre that took place on 24th May 1896, but we have gone through a more anxious time since then.

A few months after the catastrophe, a lull came; people were getting over their fright. The majority had returned to their homes, those who had olive trees had gathered their crops, and with the proceeds they had even begun to repair their houses. But the lull was of short duration. It began to be known that the Sultan had been sending emissaries to the island to encourage the Moslems to keep up the disturbances, so as to baulk the Council of Europe, whose Commissioners were then sitting. The Consuls found out that the Pasha recently sent from Constantinople had been countenancing the intrigues, so they wrote to their respective ambassadors who insisted on his recall. I think it was just about this time that a placard was posted in the streets of Canea, of which the following is a translation :

'BRETHREN. The voice of the Prophet calls to avenge ourselves against these unbelievers, who swear against our holy religion and to slay all those unbelieving Christians who have drunk of the blood of our brethren for so many years and are not yet satisfied. To arms, punish these unjust servants of our nation. By doing so you can meet our Prophet with honour'

You can easily understand that the Moslems were greatly excited by such words and began to rush towards the Christian quarter to which they set fire. You know my uncle's house is close to the Turkish arsenal at Suda bay, where all the men-of-war anchor. It is now several years since the captains of some British ships asked my uncle to allow a flagstaff to be put up on his premises for the convenience of their telegrams when the ships were in bay. My uncle, ever willing to do anything for his countrymen or his government, allowed the staff to be put up, so when the various ships came in they used to send a flag and lantern to us. The telegrams came by special messenger from Canea, three miles away, and when they reached us we hoisted the flag by day and the lantern by night, on seeing which the captain would send one of his men to take the telegrams. When the ships left Suda bay they took their signals with them, and the next that came brought their own.

But at the end of 1896 so many ships were coming and going and the telegrams became so numerous, that the captain in command thought it better to rent a house on shore and take in the wire and get a clerk from Canea to work it.

So uncle found a house for him, but the messages were still sent here. Later on they used to send one of their men to our house who transmitted the messages by signals, using flags by day and the lantern by night, and having a slate by his side with the messages written on it.

But to begin with my story. On Monday morning the 1st of February 1897, our servant came up to my room to tell me there was something wrong, for all our neighbours were in the courtyard in a state of great excitement. I went down as quick as I could without disturbing uncle and aunt, as it was still very early. When they saw me they all cried for the master. I told them he was not up yet, and even if he were, what could he do for them, unless it was to tell them to return to their homes and keep quiet.

I went outside the gate, but could only see a few Turkish officers, and when I enquired of them they said they knew nothing. Soon however we learned that the day before the Turks had committed some murders, and the Christians were all in a panic, as the Turks were openly saying in Canea that they would kill every Christian they could lay their hands on.

A man on horseback came galloping from Canea to Suda, passing through all the villages, urging the people to fly for their lives to the mountains. Many went at once, without my uncle seeing them, but a good number stayed behind. Later in the day we had a note from Captain Custance, commanding HMS Balfour then lying in the bay.

He asked uncle if he would take in six Maltese who had come for refuge alongside the ship, and could not be induced to leave. Uncle sent word at once that he would take them in. These poor men lived in Canea but they had rented a small place in Suda, in order to take in washing from the ships. A short time later, Captain Custance called to thank us for taking in the Maltese, and also to tell us he was just going to Canea, as things had a very threatening look there. We asked him what we were to do, and he said, "I am looking after you all. The Dragon will be left here, and I expect the Scout in Suda bay tomorrow". The Dragon I may tell you is a torpedo boat destroyer. We had one of her men in our house on Monday night to send off any messages.

A message came from the Scout in Canea saying she was urgently wanted there, but she was ordered to come to Suda bay at once, and the Dragon to take her place in Canea, as she could enter the harbour in rough weather more easily. So the Scout came here on Tuesday morning, and two men from her were sent on shore at once. We had then to bid our guard of Monday night goodbye and welcome our new ones. Things by this time were looking very serious.

The clerk at the telegraph station refused to remain at his post, unless he was protected by men from the Scout, as bullets were flying in every direction. Captain Noel of the Scout, followed by a man with the Union Jack unfurled, came on shore to ask uncle what he thought would be best to be done. So after consulting with uncle he sent an officer with six men to the telegraph station, and hoisted the British ensign. That same day a French ship came in to the bay and landed the same number of men and an officer who were constantly on watch, while the officer kept going to and from the telegraph station. In this way we knew what was going on in Canea. The Christian quarters of the town were in flames and matters were getting worse and worse.

On Thursday evening the officer came with a message to be signalled to the ship, 'Fire still increasing. Consuls taken refuge on board European ships stationed in Canea'. On Friday the Captain came on shore to ask us to go on board, as he thought things would get still worse, but uncle refused to leave. That same night a message came to the Scout from the Balfour – 'Break up the telegraph station and all instruments on board, embark Mr Lindsay and all within his gates'. Again uncle refused to go. They broke up the telegraph station and all came to our house that night, but for three days before that we had five men constantly with us.

Early on Saturday morning Captain Noel came ashore again to plead with my uncle to go on board, as he could not leave men on shore any longer, his senior officer had given orders that they were all to be taken on board.

But uncle said that unless things got worse, he would not leave the place, but all the refugees, numbering 45, and my aunt and I could, if we cared to. We did not care to go, in a crisis like this we decided we would all go together or stay together trusting our Heavenly Father to pull us through.

So early on Saturday morning we said goodbye to kind-hearted Captain Noel, his officers and men. They took all the refugees with them except two old women, who begged to stay with us. The rest went off under the shadow of the Union Jack, with their faces lifted towards heaven, praying God to shower down his best blessing on the Englishman's house.

When the men from the Scout left, the French followed and we were left alone; but before Captain Noel went away he saw to it that the Union Jack was hoisted on our flag staff, where it long remained night and day.

It is in our possession still, and will be kept as a memento of a time I should never go through again, but to go on with my narrative.

Our good friends from the Scout were not more than half an hour away when they came back again. A large yacht had come in to the bay. Captain Noel consulted with its owner (one of the Rothschilds), telling him he was very anxious about us now there was no telegraphic communication with Canea.

The owner very kindly said that if Captain Noel would write to Captain Custance, the yacht would go round to Canea with the letter and bring back the answer. So the men were sent back to us till the answer should come.

The yacht returned about midnight with the answer : 'If Mr Lindsay will not go on board, the men must, I cannot leave them ashore to be killed.'

So early on Sunday morning again we said goodbye to our kind friends and to make things worse, the Scout was ordered to sea, and to sea it went. We do not know how far she went. We did not ask nor did they say. But we think they only went round to Canea, where the two captains had to talk.

We do not know for certain, but a few days later Captain Custance sent a message to uncle and I believe it appears in many papers, telling him he was a brave old Scotsman, having the pluck to stay on in his house when all the Consuls had taken refuge on board the European ships, and the Scout ordered to sea.

After the men left on Sunday morning, I lay down for a short time while uncle kept watch, for our man servant had gone off to join the insurgents. When I got up, uncle lay down. But I was no sooner downstairs when the two women told me that some men had broken in to one of our small houses just outside our gate. These houses uncle lets out and the one broken in to had been abandoned the day before by people who had taken refuge on the Scout. So I went out at once and found a Turkish soldier standing outside, guarding the door, which had been forced open. I asked him what he was doing, did he know this was an Englishman's property, who would at once let the Commander of the arsenal know what he was doing. He just stood and stared at me. I was alone, for the old women would not venture outside the gate for the world. Every house by this time had been broken in to and Turkish soldiers along with Cretan Turks were carrying off property as fast as they could.

I thought he had not understood my Turkish, of which I speak very little, so I called one of the native Turks in Greek to come for a moment. He shouted back that he was too busy – busy robbing a poor widow's house. I pleaded with him to come, and at last he did and told the soldier he had better get away or it would be bad for him. So the soldier went inside, shutting the door to keep me out, but I knew he couldn't leave the house any other way, as the windows on the other side looked in to our garden. He opened the door when they had done their work, I say they, for when I got inside there were four of them making for the door with guns in their hands. They had ransacked every trunk and every corner of the house.

What they did not want was scattered about, what they wanted they had stuffed into a large bedcover, which one of the men was carrying on his back. You can understand my feelings better than I can express them. There I was alone, perfectly helpless, while they were carrying on their pillage. I tried with all my might to pull the bundle off the man's back, but failed, as you can imagine.

I managed to pull a few articles out of it when one of them lifted the butt of his gun against me. My limbs were shaking under me, but I shook my finger in his face, called them cowards, and said I was an English woman and no coward like them. But the most galling thing for me was to stand there and see them go off with their bundle.

When I got back to the house and told my story to uncle, he went off at once to the Commander of the arsenal, and told him all that had happened.

This man was indignant that any of the Sultan's soldiers should be accused of having entered any house by force. But all the same, it was known to everyone that most of the Christians' houses at Suda, none of which are far from the Sultan's arsenal, were forced by Turkish soldiers, and the plunder carried by them in to the arsenal, while the officers were looking.

The work of destruction and pillage went on for many days. First the doors, shutters and window frames were carried away, and the tiles. The men using crowbar, hammer, axe and saw, till they left the houses in a heap of ruins.

I am speaking of houses which were too near Turkish property to be set on fire. Away from such property the soldiers were satisfied with burning

These things we saw with our own eyes day after day, and yet in reading some of our own newspapers later we realised how little of what actually happened was known. One day my uncle was so angry when he saw two widows' houses knocked down, he went to one of the officers and pleaded hard for these two widows' houses to be spared. The answer he got was "Are they touching your property ? No, you say. Then you rest and be thankful. When your property is touched the blame will be on our heads." So we just had to look on and do nothing to save them. We were exposed for weeks to shot and shell flying around us, and almost every room in the house had panes of glass broken with the vibration of big guns. Had my uncle left the house as he was urged to do, it would be safe to say it would have shared the same fate as those of our poor neighbours.

I am sure it will be interesting to you and your friends to know how we fared for provisions the weeks we had the refugees and could not get anything to buy. Well, in the first place, the French man-of-war and the Scout sent us some biscuits, and the Scout whatever they had left over from their mess, while they themselves were driven to live on salt and tinned meat and biscuits.

The owner of the yacht too, very kindly sent us a large barrel of cabin biscuits and two loaves of bread, all of which we were glad to get.

Almost every year around Christmas we got a box of provisions from home, and had received one some weeks earlier. Amongst other things we had oatmeal, barley, tea, butter and cheese, the meal came in very useful. As for bread, for eight years we had not made our own, but used to get it by carrier from Canea daily, but latterly it had been so bad we thought to make it at home again. So the last week in January, uncle bought a sack of flour and we had only one baking out of it when the troubles began. We had also bought a goat with two little kids. We had got the goat for the milk, which is scarce and dear in winter. Cow's milk is never used in Crete, only that of sheep and goats.

I tell you these little incidents, to show you how our Heavenly Father was watching over us and providing many comforts for us, that otherwise we must have wanted for a long time. We also had plenty of hens at that time, and we were well supplied with fresh eggs. Many a basketful went on board the Scout when she was back again with us. One Sunday morning on her arrival, her anchor was not yet dropped when the captain came ashore and said, " I will be on your house night and day". He explained how we could communicate with the ship in the daytime and gave us rockets in case of danger at night and he turned the searchlight on our house for fifteen minutes every two hours for several nights. It is impossible to say too much of the kindness shown by Captain Noel, his officers and men. We shall never forget it.

We were a month and some days prisoners within our gates. By that time Admiral Harris and other European admirals had come to the island. Their ships came round from Canea to Suda, a distance of some sixteen knots, while patrols of troops guarded the road between the two places, which by land are only three miles apart. Then by degrees carriages began to be seen on the road and we could go back and forth to Canea in safety.

European troops soon followed and you know what has happened since. There is great distress on the island, both amongst Moslems and Christians, both of who are praying for an end of their troubles.

The Revenge, flagship of Rear-Admiral Harris, returned to Suda bay a few weeks ago. She was away for three months, as the crew required a change. The Admiral, I am sorry to say, tells us he will soon leave Crete. We are very sorry, because he has been so kind and attentive to us since he arrived, which was in March 1897. Our Seaforth Highlanders left Crete some time ago, and they were relieved by the Welsh Fusiliers, who are still here.

Five of the Seaforth Highlanders are buried in the British cemetery in Suda. More may have died in Canea, where a larger number of them were stationed. One of them, who died, was a fine young sergeant. His wife and little daughter arrived in Crete a few days before his death. He was in hospital when they came. Poor thing we all felt so sorry for her, but what a comfort it will be for her in years to come that she was able to nurse her husband in his last illness, and that she saw him laid in his grave. She spent the last few days in Crete with us, and went to the cemetery to have a last look. She is now living with her father in Durham, and has written to us twice from there. We have promised to look after her husband's grave as long as we are here and to send her a leaf or flower from it now and then. Perhaps this little pamphlet may fall in to the hands of someone who has lost a loved one from the ranks of our Seaforth Highlanders, who is now at rest in the British cemetery in Suda till the resurrection morn. It may cheer them to know that a true-hearted Scotsman in Crete attended all their funerals and saw them laid in their last resting place. The Scotch blood leapt in his veins on hearing the familiar Scottish tune played by the pipers, when following the body to the grave.

He changed the words thus :

'The bonnie flowers are blooming o'er five Hieland sod. The five little crosses mark the spot where they lie. While on earth they marched to bagpiping orders, and now their souls have gone aloft to soar above the sky. When God shall send the message forth to leave their bed of clay.'

I am sorry to say that the bones of the native Christians were not always allowed to rest in peace, which many of our British officers can testify to, who have witnessed scenes too revolting to put in print.

I will finish this letter, by offering up our heartfelt thanks and gratitude to our Heavenly Father, for his loving kindness and tender mercy to us, during the times we passed through trial and danger. We thank him for the kind friends he sent to us in our time of need, whose faces we may never see again on earth, but while memory lasts we shall always think lovingly of.

We have much, very much to be thankful for. Only our Father in Heaven knows what we have gone through since May 1896. When our refugees were with us and again the following February and for the days when bread could not be had even for gold, we never knew what want was, nor did anyone within our gates ever have cause to say they were hungry. Like the widow of Zeruphath, our barrel of meal wasted not, neither did our cruise of oil fail, as long as we needed it.

Thus far his arm has led us on. Thus far we make His mercy known, And while we tread this desert land, New mercies shall new songs demand.

I take this opportunity of publicly thanking the many friends who responded to our appeal on behalf of the poor people. By means thus placed at our disposal, we have been able to help many of our destitute neighbours, both Christian and Moslem. Whatever profit this little publication may bring, will be devoted to the same purpose. God in his love and mercy grant that peace may soon reign in this beautiful but unfortunate island, and may all things work together for man's good and His glory.

I cannot conclude without begging you to express my heartfelt thanks to my honoured minister, Mr Daly, for having so kindly advocated the cause of the poor Cretans from the pulpit. He and other friends, who have had compassion on them, will ever be remembered in our prayers.

Ever sincerely yours
Maggie Montgomery